T5-BBP-602

1

WAITING FOR THE SON

POETICS / THEOLOGY / RHETORIC
IN MARGARET AVISON'S *SUNBLUE*

BY

C.D. MAZOFF

Cormorant Books

The author and publisher wish to thank The Canada Council
and the Ontario Arts Council for their support.

Cover from an oil on canvas *eclosion* by Anne-Marie Bost,
courtesy of the artist and The Canada Council Art Bank.

Published in Canada by Cormorant Books,
RR 1, Dunvegan, Ontario K0C 1J0.
Printed in Winnipeg by Hignell Printing.

Printed and bound in Canada.

Canadian Cataloguing in Publication Data

Mazoff, Chaim David, 1949-
   Waiting for the son : poetics/theology/rhetoric
in Margaret Avison's *sunblue*

Includes bibliographical references.
ISBN 0-920953-21-2

1. Avison, Margaret, 1918-   Sunblue.
2. Avison, Margaret, 1918-   —Criticism and
interpretation. I. Title.

PS8501.V5Z77 1989   C811' .54   C89-090364-6
PR9199.3.A93Z77 1989

for Jean Cypher

TABLE OF CONTENTS

PREFACE

This volume is envisaged as a complement to the two already existing volumes of criticism on Avison's work: *Margaret Avison,* by Ernest Redekop and *Lighting up the terrain,* edited by David Kent. Redekop's work was written before Avison had published *sunblue,* and, although an excellent volume, is necessarily limited in scope. Kent's work, while being quite helpful, does not, in my opinion, do justice to Avison's intentions in *sunblue.* The articles, while engaging and informative, nevertheless do not present the reader with a unified view of Avison's poetic.

The above said, it is hoped that the lover of Avison's poetry and those interested, perhaps, in the problem of a Christian poetic will find this volume a useful addition. If it appears polemical at times, my justification is that it is time to set the record straight. To read Avison without properly accounting for her theology, her rhetoric and her poetics would be an injustice. To continue to deny *sunblue* its place in Canadian poetry, unforgiveable. This being the case, I can only hope that my prose yields as much to the reader, in its way, as does Avison's verse.

ACKNOWLEDGEMENTS

I would like to thank several people, in particular, without whose support this work would never have been possible: Gary Geddes, for the many valuable insights he has given me, as well as for the presence of his poetic ear and his sense of humour; Robert Feinstein for encouragement and guidance in matters philosophical and theological; Michael Brian for an introduction to rhetorical analysis; Wynne Francis and Bob Sorfleet for critical introductions to Margaret Avison. Finally, special thanks to Peter Aitkens, Gordon Mastine and Magali Thomas for reading the manuscripts, and to Jan Geddes for putting it all together.

REFERENCES

The references to Margaret Avison's poetry in this work are as follows: *WS/D* for the combined volume *Winter Sun/ The Dumbfounding*, and *s* for poems from *sunblue*.

All references to the Bible are taken from the King James Version.

INTRODUCTION

My own introduction to Margaret Avison came in 1983. At that time, I was an undergraduate at Concordia University feeling rather overwhelmed by the new movements in poetry and the postmodern theories that accompanied them. I was also exhausted by the bleakness and solipsism of much of modern Canadian writing. What was needed was some modern poetry that had as its purpose the recuperation of meaning, and which manifested a positive feeling about life, and humanity in general. Something that would not only delight, but also instruct, that would satisfy my spiritual needs and help point the way to integrating my intellectual knowledge with life in the real world. A poetry which even *acknowledged* a real world. Wynne Francis and Bob Sorfleet suggested Margaret Avison. I read her, and got a headache.

I have to admit that it wasn't until graduate school, when I had developed patience and a love of language, that I began to appreciate Avison's very special brand of poetry. The difficulty inherent in reading Avison's poetry has always served as a basis for criticism of her work—including my own—but a positive one; for underneath the work, hidden in its very fabric, Avison's art lies ready for the reader. This ability of Avison's, to write with the compactness and precision of the metaphysical poets, as witnessed in her sonnet, "Tennis" (*WS/D*, 26), for example, is one of her hallmarks, and has endeared her to many. Unfortunately, the other side of metaphysical poetry, its religious component, serves as a cause for discomfort when it situates itself in the present, challenges the very precepts of our modernity, and becomes something more than venerable and antique—previously safe because viewed at a distance—by intruding upon our all too comfortable, cynical solipsisms.

Margaret Avison has produced a remarkable body of work. She is, arguably, Canada's most subtle and accomplished poet, whose work may be compared with that of Herbert, Hopkins, or Yeats. And yet comparatively little has been written about her work, partially because she has been personally reticent, preferring to write poems rather than to *be the poet,* and partially because she has not been prolific, producing only five volumes of poetry and a small body of uncollected pieces.[1] However, a small output and an absence of self-promotion may be less significant in explaining the modest critical attention paid to her work than the fact of her Christian themes and orientation. Many secular critics cannot comfortably deal with deeply religious writing: either they will denigrate the religious component as ideological intrusiveness, downplay its importance, by discussing the religious element as something that is merely decorative or pretend that it is further evidence of the lingering presence of Romanticism—a philosophy which, for some, is best not taken too seriously in our most postmodern of times.

I am reminded of something Saul Bellow said in "The Gonzaga Manuscripts" about the purpose of modern literature:

> ... think first of modern literature as a sort of
> grand council considering what mankind should
> do next, how they should fill their mortal time,
> what they should feel, what they should see, where
> they should get their courage, how they should
> love, how they should be pure or great, and all the
> rest. This advice of literature has never done much
> good. But you see God doesn't rule over men
> as he used to, and for a long time people haven't
> been able to feel that life was firmly attached
> at both ends so that they could stand confidently

in the middle and trust the place where they
were. . . .²

Well, what happens when someone comes along and
says that God does rule over men, that He hasn't absconded,
but has been willingly banished; that we need no longer
continue "dreaming of some alternative to spring"—that
"Since Lucifer, waiting is all / A rebel can" (*WS/D,* 34) do, no
longer applies. In literary circles, we expect such sentiments
from Hopkins's, Herbert, and Donne, and forgive them in
Eliot. But generally, we consider them outmoded.
    This critical stance, that the religious element detracts
from and enfeebles her artistry, has produced a negative
response to Avison's Christian verse. But such criticism is
really unfounded. As Redekop, Kertzer and Doerkson³,
among others, point out, when we look back at Avison's early
work, the allusions to the struggle for meaning, to God,
religion, and alienation are clearly obvious; the biblical tropes
easily discernable under the surface of the poems, the intertex-
tuality always already there. What is one to make of poems,
such as "The Apex Animal," (*WS/D,* 11) or "Dispersed Titles"
(*WS/D,* 13), early poems which make liberal use of scriptural
allusion?⁴ Perhaps it is not this intertexuality with the Bible
that raises the ire of many a critic, but the tone that Avison's
more recent poetry manifests toward the condition of our
being in the world. A look at two poems, one early and one
late, should clarify this point. The first poem, "Not the Sweet
Cicely of Gerardes Herball" (*WS/D,* 22), contains abundant
references to biblical narratives, but it also carries a note of
despondency, and a yearning for a return to a past that can
never be: the cry of modern man experiencing his "living
darkness."

> Myrhh, bitter myrrh, diagonal,
> Divides my gardenless gardens
> Incredibly as far as the eye reaches
> In this falling terrain.
> Low-curled in rams-horn thickets,
> With hedge-solid purposefulness

It unscrolls, glistening,
Where else the stones are white,
Sky blue.
No beetles move. No birds pass over.
The stone house is cold.
The cement has crumbled from the steps.
The gardens here, or fields,
Are weedless, not from cultivation but from
Sour unfructifying November gutters,
From winds that bore no fennel seeds,
Finally, from a sun purifying, harsh, like
Sea-salt.
The stubbled grass, dragonfly-green,
Between the stones, was not so tended.
Mild animals with round unsmiling heads
Cropped unprotested, unprotesting
(After the rind of ice
Wore off the collarbones of shallow shelving rock)
And went their ways.
The bitter myrrh
Cannot revive a house abandoned.
Time has bleached out the final characters
Of a too-open Scripture.
Under the staring day
This rabbinical gloss rustles its
Leaves of living darkness.
With the maps lost, the voyages
Cancelled by legislation years ago,
This is become a territory without name.
No householder survives
To marvel on the threshold
Even when the evening myrrh raises
An aromatic incense for
Far ivory nostrils
Set in the vertical plane of ancient pride.

The second poem, "March" (s, 26), carries only one clear
allusion to anything religious, in this case to the Eucharist
("earth-loaf, sky-wine"), but is actually less textually "bibli-

10

cal" than the earlier work; however, it carries with it a spiritual confidence typical of the believer and distasteful to the confirmed cynic.

> A Caribbean airflow
> shampoos the brook.
> The deepsea deepwarm look of
> sky wakes green below
> amid the rinds of snow.
>
> Though all seems melt and rush,
> earth-loaf, sky-wine,
> swept to bright new horizons
> with hill-runnel, and gash,
> all soaked in sunwash,
>
> far north, the ice
> unclenches, booms
> the chunks and floes, and river brims
> vanish under cold fleece:
> the floods are loose!
>
> Then sullen torn
> old skies through tattery trees
> clack, freezing
> stiffens loam; the worn
> earth's spillways then relearn
> > how soaring bliss
> > and sudden-rigoring frost
> > release
> > without all lost. (s, 26)

As well as the religious component, there has always been a strong pragmatic aspect to Avison's poetry, as evidenced by her poems about social injustice, poverty and political repression—issues which move her poetry beyond the printed page. Avison's poetry, relying on the full complement of artistic devices is not merely aesthetic, not merely intellectual, political or religious, but subsumes all of these elements and links them through the poet's voice with the concrete world of experience and the senses. It is perhaps here that Avison's earlier association with Cid Corman and the projective verse of the Black Mountain School comes to the fore: her verse striving to be "kinetic rather than static . . . written in a form that projects or carries the kinetics of content, rather than molding them to a fixed pattern. . . . [A] process rather than a formally developed single perception."[5]

While some attention has been paid to Margaret Avison's first two volumes, *Winter Sun* and *The Dumbfounding,* much less has been said about her most recent collection of poems, *sunblue,* since its publication in 1978. Apart from a few reviews, one major article devoted to it, and one collection of essays, more than half of the poems in the volume have yet to be discussed.[6]

Certainly *sunblue* has had a mixed reception, owing largely to its explicitly Christian orientation; but this critical coolness is unfair, and it is the issue of this unfairness that this work intends to address by examining Avison's poetry in *sunblue* and showing how her poetics and theology work together, rather than against each other, to provide a rich experience for the reader. One is reminded of the critical reception of her second collection, *The Dumbfounding,* which clearly authenticated the genuiness of both the search and the discovery so clearly perceptible in *Winter Sun,* and of the religious quality evident in most of Avison's early, "pre-Christian" poetry.

The majority of poems in *sunblue* are concerned both with the secret life of things in a world moving towards a fusion of what James Merrett identifies as the "holy and the day-to-day," and with the description of a reality that is sacramental and whose "surface jumble is nonetheless an outward expression of inward Grace."[7] To use Martin Turnell's terminology in *Modern Literature and Christian Faith,* Avison is, like Chaucer and others before her, "interested primarily in things" and her poems are "record[s] of [her] reactions to them. The balance of the poem[s] comes from the close correspondence between emotion and the object which evokes it."[8] And, as Turnell says of Hopkins, "there is something essentially vital and alive about [her] description of nature: a sense of things living and growing."[9] This, of course, is due to Avison's sacramental view of nature: nature as "an outward and temporal sign of an inward and enduring grace."[10]

Behind many of the poems, and perhaps the guiding theme of *sunblue* itself, is the idea of the whole of creation earnestly awaiting its "adoption" by, and "redemption" in, Christ (Romans 8:18-23). The theme of release permeates the volume:

> In the sunward sugarbush
> runnels shine and down-rush
> through burning snow and thicket-slope.
> The spiced air is ocean-deep.
>
> Melting ridge and rivermouth
> shape the waters in the earth
> and the motions of the light
> close the flow as watertight.
>
>> "In and out the windows"
>> squirrels flip and play
>> through sunsplash and high and low
>> in winter's gallery.
>
> The extraordinary beyond the hill
> breathes   and is   imperturbable.
> Near the gashed bough the hornets fur
> in paperpalace-keep and -choir.
>
> Across snowmush and sunstriped maples
> honeyed woodsmoke curls and scrolls.
> Sunblue and bud and shoot wait to unlatch
> all lookings-forth, at the implicit touch.

("Released Flow," *s*, 24)

"SKETCH: Thaws," "SKETCH: A work gang on Sherbourne," "SKETCH: Cement worker on a hot day," "Stone's Secret,"

"Hid Life," "Released Flow," "March Morning," "March,"
"Highway in April," "Let Be," "Water and Worship," "The
Bible to be Believed," and "Light (II)," for example, all, as
George Johnston suggests, "deal specifically with thaws, with
'Released Flow,' with the revelations of 'Hid Life'."[11] It is the
release of the hidden life of the self into a sacramental
wholeness to which these poems allude. Images of cleansing
also abound, symbolized by water and by light; images of
fertility and fruition, symbolized by allusions to a graced
nature and to the colour green; and images of communion (the
Eucharist).[12] The interplay of light and shadow, of transparency and opacity, occurs regularly throughout, pointing as it
does to the struggle within man for meaning in the face of
alienation, and to the possibility of wholeness in Christ as it
has been revealed in the Bible. Some mention has been made
about Avison's seeming pre-occupation with death in *sunblue,* interpreting such references as morbid.[13] However,
Avison's musings on mortality serve not only as *memento
mori* to a mechanized mankind careening across the universe,
as in "Kahoutek," and to the babbling engineers squalling at
each other in "Technology is Spreading," but also as reminders to us of both the difficulties of language and our finitude.

> The Comet
> among us sun and planets
> I saw with naked eye, i.e.
> nothing between my ice-
> > keening
> > tear-washed
> > seeing
> > from earth-mound (here) to
> ocean-deep navy-blue out-there (there).
> > In the traffic-flow
> > a frozen lump
> > from a jolting fender
> > spins meteor-black
> > towards the midwinter bus-stop where I stand
> > under the tall curved night.

Veering weird-brightness
from somewhere else:
we solar-system people flinch
                    as at a doom-sign,
and find you cryptic
          from far unlanguaged precincts
              soundlessly hollowing past us.

My tongue, palate, lips, teeth, life's breath,
pronounce "comet", call off
as told
how many million miles away
I with the naked eye still-standing see
you, it—
of quite another orbit.

                              ("Kahoutek," *s*, 90)

    The many references to travel in *sunblue* reflect Avi-
son's concern with the pilgrim's progress—with the journey
of life itself. *sunblue*'s many references to the wilderness
experience of the "chosen," that is, the "Church," as well as to
faith in the face of seemingly insurmountable obstacles, such
as the slough of despond of twentieth-century Canadian life,
point to the actuality of the wilderness experience in the life of
the Christian and the non-Christian alike, as well as to the
relevancy of the biblical narratives to the contemporary situation. Avison's thematics—politics, ecology, unemploy-
ment, alienation—clearly give her work a postmodern fla-
vour; moreover, her concern over perception and language, as
well as her preoccupation with origins and the trace, recalls the
philosophies of both Jacques Derrida and Emmanuel Levinas,
and reflects, what deconstruction calls, the infinite play of the
signifier.
    Finally, *sunblue* is a joyous celebration of the life in
Christ that is conveyed through Avison's "careful observation
of minutiae,"[14] by the power of her language,[15] and by her
powerful "optic heart,"[16] whose focus is the moving towards
"the sacramental re-possession of nature and time, things, and

history"[17]—the restoration of all things in Christ.[18]

This work deals with *sunblue* in three main sections—Release, In the Strong Sun, and Restoration—and it pays particular attention to the many poems that have not yet been discussed in print.

I will try to show how, by the use of specific strategies, Avison draws the participant in her work into that special ground between reader and text, a place which contemporary poetics argues does not exist (deconstruction), knowledge (phenomenology), or reduces to word-play (structural linguistics), but which Christianity sees as a place of sacramental presence. By exploiting what Iser calls the asymmetry between text and reader and by use of a repertoire (of technical procedures, strategies)[19] which draws heavily on the Christian biblical tradition, projective verse techniques, and rhetorical legerdemain, Avison attempts to engage the reader in a sacramental experience beyond the text itself by making full use of the reader's own "stock of experience."[20]

Avison's theology, and in particular her Christology— that is, her understanding of the nature and the person of Christ—is Pauline rather than Johannine, more Judaeo-Christian than Hellenist-Christian. Its emphasis is on the spiritual life *in* this world, rather than in the one to come, and its conception of Christ focusses on his humanity and suffering, rather than on his divinity and glorification. Its emphasis is also on the ethical, rather than solely upon the noumenal dimension of the spiritual life, and thus speaks strongly about the human will, reflecting an existential orientation that recalls Tillich's theology of "ultimate concern." Avison's theology is also a "limited natural theology,"[21] rather than a purely "natural theology," in that, although it acknowledges the revelation of God in creation, it nevertheless posits the necessity of a "special revelation" needed to understand His grace:

> God (being good) has let me know
> no good apart from Him.
> He, knowing me, yet promised too
> all good in His good time.

This light, shone in, wakened a hope
that lives in here-&-now—

("Oughtiness Ousted," *s,* 64)

The above distinctions are essential to a proper understanding of Avison's poetry, since without them, the focus of many of her poems becomes unclear, and the reader may, as Kertzer and others seem to do, equate the aesthetic with the ontological, which, in her case, would be to miss the point of her poetry.[22] For Avison, Salvation and the Incarnation are not merely aesthetic experiences—for example, metaphors for some higher type of "felt" experience—but ontological ones. For Avison, Christ "was flesh; was there" (*WS/D,* 146). To see Avison's poetry as "intrinsically *literary*"[23] would be to miss the point altogether: it would interpret Avison's allusions to Christianity as devices that help make the poems "work," rather than as strategies whose intentions are to lead the reader into an encounter with the Holy itself. Avison's poetry in *sunblue* is intended to be "a window through which other entities can be perceived,"[24] and those entities are God and, what Paul Weiss calls, "existence affected" by Him.[25]

Having seen too many interpretations that have used the aesthetic object to support untenable theories, I have decided to approach *sunblue* from its beginning: from what I consider to be the author's intention. Which is not to say that I am ignoring the "intentional fallacy," but that I believe that E.D. Hirsch Jr. is correct both when he raises the question as to who exactly the author is, and when he points out the dangers of the critic and not the author being the arbiter of meaning.[26]

A perfect example of critic as author can be seen, for instance, in Klus's claim that *The Dumbfounding,* unlike *Winter Sun,* is

a highly structured book. It begins with poems set
in spring and ends with poems set in fall with an
anticipation of approaching winter. There is,

17

besides, a central group of 22 poems concerning Christian revelation and the Christian life. These poems are set, appropriately enough, in summer, and, as Tillinghast notes, "are modestly placed in the middle of the book, so that one discovers them gradually." "Searching and Sounding," describing the actual moment of revelation and thus the climactic moment of the book, is set in the heat of July.[27]

One might then, go on, as many have, to conclude that Avison's purpose in writing *The Dumbfounding* was to furnish the world with a description of her "own very personal spiritual experience."[28] The fact is that Avison intended nothing of the sort:

I didn't decide any such thing! I had the writing done (in odd moments, at a familiar nudging to explore this edge-of-field-of-vision-glide of meaning to get rid of the distraction of it too). And then Denise Levertov wrote me from New York that Norton wanted 6 poets (to use up some advertising money on a "prestige PR project,") so I sent the book along for her to read and they published it.[29]

One may choose to see *The Dumbfounding* as Avison's Christian manifesto, but she declares this not to be the case. One may also believe like Klus that "Searching and Sounding" is the poem which describes the moment of conversion, or, like Jones and myself, that it is "Person."[30]

Redekop uses a similar argument for "The Bible to be Believed" in *sunblue,* seeing this poem as the apex of the volume, while McNally traces a seasonal arrangement in *sunblue* that is similar to the one Klus perceives in *The Dumbfounding.*[31] One might even see in *sunblue* an arrangement along a liturgical cycle, or see the volume itself as an extended sketch, in that it is framed between SKETCH poems. However, dividing the volume up into such categories should serve merely as a heuristic device.

18

My intention being *not* to force yet another interpretation on an unsuspecting reader, I have decided to focus on three specific areas of Avison's poetry: her typology, that is, her system of biblical interpretation, since it is a major component of her repertoire; the effect and the importance of her theology, which I try to demonstrate is Pauline and not Johannine; and her use of rhetoric, those skills and strategies that she uses both to destabilize the text and to defamiliarize the reader.

Chapter One, "Release," comprises a study of the themes and techniques of *sunblue,* with special attention being paid both to a discussion of Avison's use of typology and poetic technique, and also to her soteriology (her understanding of salvation), and ontology (her understanding of what it means to be human). In Chapter Two, "In the Strong Sun," the discussion broadens out to include an investigation of Avison's epistemology (her theory of knowledge), and the ramifications of her expressly Pauline theology, while still focussing closely on her poetic technique. In Chapter Three, "Restoration," the implications of Avison's eschatology (her understanding of prophesy and the world to come) are discussed, and conclusions are made about the volume, and Avison's Christian poetic.

CHAPTER ONE

RELEASE

For we know that the whole creation groaneth and
travaileth in pain together until now. And not only
they, but ourselves also, which have the firstfruits
of the Spirit, even we ourselves groan within
ourselves, waiting for the adoption, to wit, the redemption of our body (Rom. 8:22-23).

"SKETCH: Thaws" (*s*, 9), the first poem in *sunblue*,
sets the tone of the volume: one of tension and release. The
arrangement on the page, the breaking up of the lines and the
use of hyphens have the effect of alternately retarding and
speeding up the reading process and create the sensation in the
reader of "thaw[ing]."

> The snowflow
> nearly-April releases   melting bright.
>
> Then a darkdown
>   needles and shells the pools.
>
> Swepth of suncoursing sky
> steeps us in
>   salmon-stream
>   crop-green

rhubarb-coloured shrub-tips:

everything waits for the
lilacs, heaped tumbling—and their warm
licorice perfume.

By the careful use of neologisms, irregular rhythms,
spondees and compound epithets, Avison is able to convey the
sensation of anticipation and release described in the poem.
The use of a spondee in the first line on the word "snowflow"
followed by a line-break creates a halting rhythm, which, in
turn, produces a sense of anticipation; this is immediately
followed by a speeding up in the second line created by falling
rhythm on "nearly-April" and then by a slowing down ef-
fected by long vowels on "releases" and by the use of space on
the page. A similar pattern is followed in the third and fourth
lines with a spondee on "darkdown," which is again followed
by a line break; the accents on "shells the pools," however,
bring the reader to an abrupt halt.
        "Melting bright" and "darkdown" followed by "shells"
evoke images of war and invite the word "meltdown"—
intense light—an idea previously conveyed by Avison in
"Searching and Sounding" (*WS/D*, 154) through the use of the
word "radium" for the purifying presence of God. "Swepth,"
a combination of sweep and depth, coming as it does after the
downward finality of "shells the pools," catches the reader up
in the "suncoursing sky," the luscious presence of God, and
"steeps us in / salmon-stream / crop-green / rhubarb-coloured
shrub-tips." Underneath all these natural images is an expression of Avison's faith; the technique used is *not* allegory,[1] but
simple, Christian typology. For example, in Christian symbolism the river (here, the "salmon-stream") is seen as the
river of life and fish as people—in fact the earliest sign used
by the Christian community to identify itself was the sign of
the fish, itself derived from the Greek anagram for Jesus Christ
Son of God Saviour (IXØYC)[2]—"crop-green" alludes to
communion,[3] while the red of "rhubarb" refers to the blood of
Christ that makes the regeneration ("green") possible. "Lilacs" connote two different symbols: if violet, they are the

symbol of suffering and of the Passion; if purple, they represent the presence of God the King. Purple, however, is also the colour for Advent and Lent, and violet/purple, appears frequently throughout the first section of *sunblue* whose main theme is preparation for Easter: release from the death of winter, release from death-in-life. "Licorice" means "sweet root" and refers to the "root of Jesse" (Isa. 11:10), the Messiah, and "perfume," to Christ, the "sweetsmelling" sacrifice (Lev. 1:9; Eph. 5:2), the means of our redemption. This last stanza is exquisite in its use of poetic technique to convey the sense of movement it describes: the accent on "heaped," the caesura between "heaped" and "tumbling," and the following dash create the sensation of "heaped tumbling," while the slow, easy rhythm and full, soft sounds of "their warm/ licorice perfume" create much the same effect as "the silver reaches of the estuary" in "The Swimmer's Moment" where, through "the falling rhythm of 'silver reaches,' followed by the preponderance of gentle stresses in 'of the estuary'," the poem transcends itself.[4] Similar Avisonian wizardry continues throughout most of *sunblue*.

This jumbling of the senses is intrinsic to Avison's poetics, a poetics that attempts to engage the reader in the poem by demanding that his "optic heart venture" forth ("Snow," *WS/D*, 27). The "process of approaching awareness by moving through particulars," however, is not only "the basis of a poetic technique,"[5] but also essential to Avison's Christianity:

> To Christian eyes, diversity is a good thing in itself, for God made diversity. He did not create "trees"; He created pines, oaks, and ginkgoes. The animals are as fantastically varied as the impish drawings of a surrealist. The temperaments of men are as varied as the forms of animals. Christianity aims not at the bypassing of individuality and absorption back into the All, but at fulfilment and redemption of the individual. Salvation is not absorption but relationship.[6]

22

The awareness that "the world is charged with the grandeur of God," and that "there lives the dearest freshness deep down things"[7] underlies and informs the poems of *sunblue*. It is, as Sallie McFague Tesselle points out, the idea that "God sustains the world, that the world is renewed by the spirit of God in spite of man's indifference to God and his destruction of the earth."[8] This is one of the themes of "SKETCH: Overcast Monday" (*s*, 11), where one is presented with what at first looks like quite a despairing picture—an image that is undone by Avison's usual complement of rhetorical devices.

> In this earth-soakt air
> we engage with
> undeathful technicalities,
> hurt that they click.
>
> An oil of gladness, in
> the seafloor Light
> quickens, secretly.

"Earth-soakt air," in the context of the first stanza, is rather straightforward. It refers to the death-in-life of modern mechanized man, "the routine matters that fill our lives and hurt us because they deny our mortality,"[9] a theme with which Avison has always wrestled and which is treated extensively in this volume. The sense is of smog-filled air, of pollution, of sin; it is paradoxical since air is up and earth is down: it refers to the Fall; it refers to man—an overabundance of man to the exclusion of God. The second stanza, however, turns the poem on its head: "Oil of gladness" is from Hebrews 1:9 and Isaiah 61:1, and refers to the promise of restoration. "Seafloor Light" can mean "see" floor, that is to say, a place of vision, and "floor," to the Ground of all Being, the ocean whence we all emerged, while "Light" refers to God, God's truth, and a physical state opposite to heavy, or "earth-soakt." The idea of see-change is an implicit reference to "Ariel's Song" in *The Tempest*,[10] where the pun on "sea" (see) evokes the spiritual dimension: there has been a change in the manner of perception, a "sea-change."

By placing the "Light" stanza under the heavy one in "Overcast Monday," Avison has destabilized the poem, and it is waiting to topple, to be "overcast." This is also reflected in the physical geography of the poem: the first stanza has four lines while the bottom one has only three. As Merrett points out, this instability is "suggested by the pun in the title. Overcast means cloudy, but also thrown over."[11]

The last line not only implies resurrection but also alludes to *Dies Illa*, the Day of the Lord. It recalls Hopkins' "it will flame out, shining like shook foil; / It gathers to a greatness, like the ooze of oil,"[12] and emphasizes God's faithfulness: the resurrection did occur, will occur and is occurring now. Man's sanctification is going on in spite of himself, since he is too preoccupied with "technicalities."

Avison takes up this idea of preoccupation with technicalities to the exclusion of life in the paired poems "SKETCH: A work gang on Sherbourne and Queen, across from a free hostel for men" (*s*, 12) and "SKETCH: Cement worker on a hot day" (*s*, 13).

> The hostel's winter flies
> where morning spills them out
> fumble, undisturbed
> by street or curb;
>
> paralleled, walled off, by the force
> of the through north-south route,
> they never meet
> the yellow-helmeted men across the street
> whose tangling ways, among
> dump trucks and crane scoops, put
> down, solid and straight,
> the new storm sewer conduit.
> Both groups go zigzag, veer,
>   stand, wait—
>
> but not the same.

The reader is immediately set off balance by the paradoxical title of the first of these poems: the working men are slaves, members of a "work gang," while the tramps who are slaves to alcohol and deprivation are "free." The reader is then further defamiliarized by the wordplay on "flies," which serves as a noun, a verb, a euphemism for the tramps and as an allusion to Gloucester's exclamation about mankind being to the gods as flies are to wanton boys.[13]

These "flies" represent people who are "walled-off" from and yet "parallel" to the people in the work gang. They are divided by a road and "they never meet."

> Both groups go zigzag, veer,
> stand, wait—
>
> but not the same.

This idea of parallel lines never meeting is discussed in "Perspective,"[14] as is the idea of a see-change.

In "Cement worker on a hot day," one of the workers manages to break free; the agent is a "yellow hydrant," "just a knob / shape," that becomes alive. There is a parable here of course: the dead word—conventional mechanized religion—takes on meaning.

> I've passed this yellow hydrant
> in sun and sleet, at dusk—
> just a knob
> shape.
>
> Now, here, this afternoon
> suddenly a man
> stops work on the new curb in
> the oils of sun,
>
> and (why of course!)
> wrenches the hydrant till
> it yields a gush
> for him to gulp and wash in.

> Yes   yes   a hydrant
> was always there but now
> it's his,   and flows.

Yellow is the colour of the Sun, which, in Avison's religious
poetry, represents Christ: God's revealed Truth,[15] while the
referent for the "hydrant" is the "fountain of living waters" of
Jeremiah 2:13. The workman has a grace experience: he is "in
/ the oils of sun," and wrestles with the hydrant, much like
Jacob with the angel (Gen. 32:24-29) until "it yields a gush /
for him to gulp and wash in":

> Yes yes a hydrant
> was always there but now
> it's his, and flows.[16]

Given both its intricate use of imagery and allusion, it
is surprising that "SKETCH: A childhood place" (*s*, 14) has
not yet been discussed in any critical works on Avison. On the
surface it is a scape poem whose theme is mortality; yet a
closer look—and *all* of Avison's poems merit closer scru-
tiny—reveals another, richer level.

> In the mattressed pasture the
> sun's butterfat
>   glistens on coarse grass.
>
> The grassblades scrape.
>
>   ...Seashells of my scattered years
>   whiten in the sun...
>
> On the weathered door
> wood-hairs leave shadow-lines on the
> hot wood.

The poem is divided into two sections. It moves progressively
from images of opulence and comfort ("mattressed pasture,"
and "sun's butterfat / glistens") to images of roughness ("coarse
grass," and "grassblades scrape"), and from images of fertility

to those of barrenness, ("Seashells of my scattered years / whiten in the sun," and "weathered door"). But if we remember that Avison uses her images consistently, and we read this poem in the light of the other poems in this volume, "SKETCH: A childhood place" assumes deeper meaning and greater poetic richness.

The "mattressed pasture" is a place that is comfortable and nourishing because of the "sun's butterfat." "Sun," here, refers to the Son as it usually does in Avison's poetry,[17] "butterfat," to the oil (grace) of the Son/milk Word of God (1 Pet. 2:2), and "coarse grass," to the natural world. "Scrape," "Seashells of my scattered years / whiten," and "shadow-lines" all indicate the passage of time. There is a change of focus as we pass to the last stanza. The narrator looks away from graced nature, the passage of time and her inner-landscape to a "weathered door"—Jesus, tried and tested: "weathered."[18] The "wood-hairs" amplify the image of humanity "on the weathered door," and carry with them an association with splinters (splinters of the Cross?) and/or the crown of thorns. The "hot wood," of course, is the Cross itself, "hot" with the blood of the Passion. The reference here is to *Dominus regnat de ligno*, (the Lord reigns from the wood [cross]). This is "the keynote of Christian resurrection."[19]

In the light of the general themes of release, Lent, and redemption in the first part of *sunblue*, this reading is not at all stretched, nor is it out of place. A New Critical reading of the poem is insufficient, since the Christian typology of Avison's poetry suggests a further, deeper level of meaning. It thus becomes obvious that the lines

> ...Seashells of my scattered years
> whiten in the sun...

refer to the valley of dry bones in Ezekiel 33, and thus indicate both the expectation of redemption and the process of purification over time as a result of exposure to the sun/Son Word.

Other poems noticeably absent from critical discussion are "SKETCH: CNR London to Toronto (I)" (*s*, 15) "SKETCH: CNR London to Toronto (II)," (*s*, 16) and "SKETCH: From train window (Leamington to Windsor) in

March" (s, 17). They share the themes of the journey of life, redemption, the optic heart and the hidden life. In "SKETCH: CNR London to Toronto (I)" the movement is away from a deformed nature, ("knock-kneed trees," "thorny" and "tilt[ed]"), to a nature that is graced: "frost / squeaky, bright with berries," in "SKETCH: CNR London to Toronto (II)." The "mo[u]rning places" of the first poem have been exchanged for the sweet "invisibility" of life "in the Christmas tree and / icing sugar country."

"SKETCH: From train window (Leamington to Windsor) in March," reveals Avison at her best. Her preoccupation with detail and her use of changing perspective combine to draw the reader both into and beyond the poem. The increasing and overwhelming clarity and focus combined with succulent language work together to create a "visual amplitude so still / that you can hear the hidden culvert gurgle."

> Miles of beeswax mist,
>   a far ravine with fishbone trees,
>   one nearer, peacock's quill-fan with
>   the violet batik faintly suggested
>   by springtime leaflessness;
>   rust-spotted chipped-paint places,
>   roadshoulder, gas-pumps, and a
>   flagless, metal flagstick;
>   somebody's bricks stashed under tarpaulins,
>   a wooden bridge in a field and a black
>   dog pottily floundering across it:
>
> the pale wintergreen air has
> straw stuck to it, and then again becomes
>   dimmed in beeswax mist, a
>   visual amplitude so still
>   that you can hear the hidden culvert gurgle.

The movement is from panoramic purity and exquisite delicacy rife with Christian symbols ("peacock," "fishbone," and "violet"),[20] to images of urban decay:

>   rust-spotted   chipped-paint places,
>   roadshoulder, gas-pumps, and a
>   flagless metal flagstick.

    The last stanza is connected to the first by an enigmatic
image of a "dog pottily floundering across" a "wooden bridge,"
which conjures up simultaneous images of drowning and
salvation as in "The Swimmer's Moment" (*WS/D* 47): the
idea of baptismal regeneration, as well as images of fullness
and even inebriation. The green in this poem is not lush but
"pale," a negative image but for the "straw stuck to it": the
straw from the manger, perhaps? The narrator returns us to the
"beeswax mist," yet the movement is not circular: "you can
hear the hidden culvert gurgle" (giggle?).   The "hidden
culvert," like the "seafloor Light" of "SKETCH: Overcast
Monday," foreshadows a change. The poem closes with an
intense expectation of joy and of blossoming: the promise of
restoration has been fulfilled; the colours will come, and
anagogic spring will arrive.
    "The Seven Birds (College Street at Bathurst):
SKETCH" (*s*, 18) and "SKETCH: End of a day: OR, I as a
blurry" (*s*, 19) are two poems that focus on the idea of wholeness (communion), or the lack of it, by emphasizing the cor-
responding presence or lack of *Mitsein* ("With-Being") in
mankind and his relationship to the world: the ability to "be-
with."[21] In "The Seven Birds," a poem relying on the techniques of Anglo-Saxon alliterative verse, images of darkness
and negativity seem to prevail; they overwhelm the "Light"
much as the sprung rhythm, compound epithets, caesuras and
alliteration of the poem combine to overwhelm the reader:

>   Storm-heaped west, wash-soaked with
>   dayspill. Light's combers
>   broken, suds-streaming
>   darkwards and stormwards

Darkness seems to have the upper hand: "Light," Christ's
presence, is overwhelmed. The predominance of negative
images ("rough," "false," and "futile"), images of danger,
implied by "High-wire," and images of neglect, conveyed by

"nobody home" and gritty children, emphasize the alienation of mechanized man who has sold his birthright for a mess of pottage, "hoping for supper" (Gen. 25:29-34). This world is barren, doubly "flat." The idea of alienation is reinforced by the allusion to "rails and wheels": "tracks that [do] not meet,"[22] and the "heavy" image of an impoverished humanity, trapped in its circus-like existence.

Nevertheless, even though heaven's presence is only a "shadow," this world still lies under "heaven," and is still subject to grace. For even as images of the apocalypse loom on the horizon, the promise of redemption is present in the images of the "pomegranate," the emblem of Easter day,[23] the "Seven birds," who call to mind the seven churches of Revelation, and the "bells" which signify both "the coming of Christ in the Eucharist" to feed those "home-bent crowds, / hoping for supper," and act as a warning to the demonic powers of the poem.[24]

In contrast to the above poem, "SKETCH: End of a day: OR, I as a blurry" portrays a world in which communion is active. Often, in *sunblue*, Avison portrays the narrator as other than human. Sometimes the narrator is a tree, as in "Hid Life," and "March Morning," or a river, as in "Water and Worship." Here, however, the narrator is a "groundhog," the emblem of the sun.[25]

> I as a blurry groundhog bundling home
> find autumn storeyed:
>
>> underfoot is leafstain and gleam of wet;
>> at the curb, crisp weed
>> thistled and russeted;
>> then there's the streetlight level;
>> then the window loftlights, yellower;
>> above these, barely, tiers
>> of gloaming branches,
>> a sheet of paraffin-pale wind,
>> then torn cloud-thatch and
>> the disappearing clear.

Indoors promises
such creatureliness as disinhabits
a cold layered beauty
flowing out there.

"SKETCH: End of a day: OR, I as a blurry" utilizes
many poetic devices to convey the richness of the images
portrayed: the rhythm of the first line conveys the ambling of
a "groundhog bundling"; the diction mixes liquids and frica-
tives richly, and employs internal rhyme, consonance, repetition and paronomasia to convey the rich texture of "autumn
storeyed." It invites the "optic heart" to zoom from the close-
up to the panoramic. "SKETCH: End of a day: OR, I as a
blurry" utilizes a framing device and thus presents both a story
within a story, and also a layered, polysemous poem, or,
"autumn storeyed." The reader is invited to see the world not
only from an animal's point of view, but also from "underfoot": the hid-life itself. The inner life is full of potential
("leafstain and gleam of wet"). However, the further away
one moves, and the more one's perspective changes as a consequence, the less hospitable this autumn harvest becomes.
Now there is "crisp weed," "thistled" and "bare"; the world is
"pale" and "torn." The movement has been away from a
stored/storied richness to the barrenness of "gloaming
branches," and the "torn cloud thatch," a movement away
from natural to technological imagery ("streetlight," "window loftlight"). The reader is conveyed from a sense of
security to an awareness of exposure to the elements. The roof
("thatch") of his autumn den has been ripped ("torn") away.

Paradoxically, however, the clearness that this exposure should bring is, somehow, not that clear at all; it is
"disappearing." One notes the inversion of the typological
order here—the sky opens out to chaos, not to the sun/Son—
and its effect of frustrating the reader's expectations.

The last stanza brings us indoors again, an indoors
strongly reminiscent of the last stanza of "New Year's Poem"
where "this unchill, habitable interior / Which mirrors quietly
the light / Of the snow" has been "won from space" (*WS/D*,
39); the difference is that in "I as a blurry" the sense of

"creatureliness" is the result of grace: nothing has been won; everything has been given.

This poem, which is powerful in its own right, gains immeasurably by its placement next to such an ostensibly dark poem as "The Seven Birds" although the syntax, sound, measure, word-play and literariness in "The Seven Birds" also act toward mitigating the darkness. Arranging the poems this way highlights the contrast between a death-in-life existence in a mechanized world and an existence in a world of graced nature, where "With-Being" (*Mitsein*) has been achieved.

Both "Stone's Secret" (*s*, 21-22) and "Hid Life" (*s*, 23) deal with the same question: Can life come to this death-in-life? Can this dead flesh, stone, river, tree regenerate?

> Botanist, does the seed
> so long up held
> still somehow inform
> petal and apple-spring-perfume
> for sure, from so far?

Or,

> Is the weight only
> a waiting

Both of these poems stress that there is a power,

> A motion and a spirit, that impels
> All thinking things, all objects of all thought,
> And rolls through all things.[26]

This power, however, is *not* some vague spirit of the mind, nor is it Nature herself. Avison makes it quite clear in her poetry that the power that rejuvenates all life, that graces nature, is the "Word" who "will come / 'like a river and the / glory . . . like a flowing stream'" ("Stone's Secret," *s*, 21-22). The Word, that by which "all things were made" (John 1:3) and in whom "we live, and move and have our being" (Acts 17:28), *is* the river of life, is Himself hidden in the river of life through all the ages, and will speak: the "Otter smooth boulder" shall "utter" (s, 21-22). The poetics involved in the otter/utter sounds should alert the reader to how Avison's mind and ear work. The sound of otter echoes through the poem in "out there," repeated three times, and finds its final variant in utter—a fine indicator of the utter importance of the ear in Avison's work. The attentive ear will also detect how she builds up the structure of repeated sounds: stilled/still/stone; skies/signal/subject; memorial/men's/mathematics; and blizzards/black/breasted/brim, for example. The alliterative component is quite noticeable in places; but, most often, it is submerged and only registers in the ear as a sort of *basso ostinato*.

This first section of *sunblue* seeks to portray what can happen when God's creation is in right relationship with Him. Spring just doesn't happen: it happens "at the implicit touch":

> The extraordinary beyond the hill
> breathes and is imperturbable.
> Near the gashed bough the hornets fur
> in paperpalace-keep and -choir.
>
> Across snowmush and sunstriped maples
> honeyed woodsmoke curls and scrolls.
> Sunblue and bud and shoot wait to unlatch
> all lookings forth, at the implicit touch
>
> ("Released Flow," *s*, 24)

The sense of the promise of fullness is conveyed by the internal rhyme, assonance and alliteration of the poem. The long open vowels, liquid, nasal and trilled consonants, and the alternation of long and short stresses combine to bring out the richness of the theme, and contribute to the smoothness of the verse. One can see a strong similarity between the luscious language and paradoxes, such as "burning snow," which is reminiscent of Wyatt's "I burn and freeze like ice," and the metaphysical conceit of the sixteenth century lyrical tradition.[27] The overwhelming sense of harmony is reflected in, and maintained by, the presence of the rhyme scheme. There is a sense of the genesis in which the hand of God "shape[d] the waters in the earth / and the motions of the light" (Gen. 1:1-10). The "sunward sugarbush" has become a house of worship; its "choir" made up of angelic "hornets," and the walls of exquisite delicacy.

"March Morning" (s, 25) is a beautiful description of the process of release that flows throughout the first section of *sunblue*:

> The diamond-ice-air is ribbon-laced
> with brightness. Peaking wafering snowbanks are
> sun-buttery, stroked by the
> rosey fingertips of young
> tree shadows
> as if for music;
> and all the eyes of God glow, listening.

> My heart branches,
> swells into bud and spray:
> heart break.

> The neighbour's kid
> lets fall his mitts
> shrugs jacket loose
> and wondering   looks   breathing the
> crocus-fresh breadwarm
> Being—
> easy as breathing.

The pun in the first line creates two images: one is of brilliantly clear and clean air ("frost squeaky") ("SKETCH: CNR London to Toronto (II)," s, 16); the other is of this "air" as "hair" laced perhaps with "beeswax mist" ("SKETCH: From train window (Leamington to /Windsor) in March," s, 17) and "shampoo[ed] by "a Caribbean airflow" ("March," s, 26). The snowbanks are as tasty and nutritious as Peak Frean wafers: they are "peaking wafering," and "sun-buttery." But the image of the sun's butter, as we saw in "SKETCH: A childhood place" (s, 14), refers to the oil of gladness, the

34

presence of the Holy Spirit, and the grace of God. The image of the "tree shadows" making "music" on the "snowbanks" evokes the Romantic image of the soul of man as an aeolian harp; here, however, the heart is the heart of the natural world. The last line of the first stanza puns on the "diamond-ice" calling it the "listening" "eyes of God."

The next stanza revolves about two implied but not spoken associations raised by the poem: that the "ice," "eyes" may also be "I's";[28] and that the aeolian harp imagery also applies to the poet—the poet as tree:

> My heart branches,
> swells into bud and spray:
> heart break.

One notes the puns on "spray" as pray and on "heart break" as joyous rupture. The sense of blossoming is powerful, evoking images of sea "spray," "melt and rush," as in the poem "March." The "rush" is a rush into the sacramental presence of God:

> earth-loaf, sky-wine,
> swept to bright new horizons
> with hill-runnel, and gash,
> all soaked in sunwash.
>
> (*s*, 26)

The above two poems ("March" and "March Morning") are central to Avison's understanding of release— release into the sacramental presence of a world infused by the grace of God, a world that naturally reflects God's grandeur and is oriented in praise towards Him—and contain echoes of other poems in this volume. We can hear "Swepth of sun-coursing sky," from "SKETCH: Thaws," in place of "swept to bright new horizons," above, and hear, as well, echoes from "Released Flow" with words such as "gash" and "runnel." "Torn / old skies through tattery trees" recalls the "torn cloud thatch and / the disappearing clear" of "End of a day," and the "crocus-fresh breadwarm / Being— / easy as breathing" of "March Morning" is transformed into a symphony of sound as the earth responds to the "sunwash" and all is reborn:

> far north, the ice
> unclenches, booms
> the chunks and floes, and river brims
> vanish under cold fleece:
> the floods are loose!
>
> Then sullen torn
> old skies through tattery trees
> clack, freezing
> stiffens loam; the worn
> earth's spillways then relearn
> > how soaring bliss
> > and sudden-rigouring frost
> > release
> > without all lost.

The message is quite clear: Spring will come, life will come, grace is here. The whole creation celebrates its redemption and moves towards communion. But just as in the Bible, where one is invited to become as a little child to receive the message of rebirth, of *Mitsein* (Matt.18:3), so also in *sunblue* the reader is presented with an alternative to "the striped, rampstripping, wireless / highway" and "all the dark inwardness" ("Highway in April," *s,* 27) of his technologically and ontologically disorientated existence:

> The neighbour's kid
> lets fall his mitts
> shrugs jacket loose
> and wondering looks breathing the
> crocus-fresh breadwarm
> > Being—
> easy as breathing.

"Being [is as] easy as breathing." All that it requires is being in the light, being in the right relationship—a receptive one—to the "implicit touch" ("Released Flow," *s,* 24).

"Water and Worship: an open-air service on the

Gatineau River" (*s*, 29) is the last poem of the spring section of *sunblue*. Its concerns are with release, the poet (humanity) as river, the hid-life, the river of life and the optic heart. A parallel is established between the river within, where

> currents within us course
> as from released snow, rock-
> sluiced, slow welling from
>   unexpected hidden springs,

and the Gatineau,

>   . . . deep,
>   cold, black, cedar-sharp.
>   The water is self-gulping.

The river's pollution, "waters still acid, / metallic with old wrecks," is thus a metaphor for pollution from sin, since the river spoken of is now both natural and spiritual. In words reminiscent of Herbert's "Love," where Love "Drew nearer to me,"[29]

>   . . . Love draws near,
>   cut-glass glory, shattering everything
>   else in
>   the one hope known:

The poet unites previously disparate images, the "mica" glinting on the "pathway" of line 1 and the "cut-glass glory" of Christ, to further unify the two seemingly unrelated halves and themes of the poem. Thus

>   The waters lap.
>   Rocks contain and wait
>   In the strong sun,

refers to both nature qua nature, and also to the people of God, the living stones of his Church (1 Cor. 3:16), who "will / wondering wait / until this very stone / utters" ("Stone's Secret," *s*, 22).

Before leaving this discussion of the first part of *sunblue*, a summary of the more important aspects of Avison's poetic as it has revealed itself might help to refresh our memories. We noted that behind many of the poems, and perhaps the guiding theme of *sunblue* itself, is the idea of the whole of the creation earnestly awaiting its "adoption" by, and its "redemption" in, Christ. This creation includes not only the secret life of things in the world but also mankind alienated from itself in a world seemingly hostile and meaningless, and yet a world informed by the grace of God: a world which is "sunblue." We noted that by the use of specific strategies, Avison draws the reader into the place between the reader and the text, a place of sacramental presence, by taking advantage of the asymmetry between the text and the reader, and that by the use of a specific linguistic repertoire, one which draws heavily on the Christian Biblical tradition, she attempts to involve the reader in an experience beyond the text itself by exhausting his storehouse of projections. She up-ends poems, puns constantly, overwhelms both language and reader alike with charged diction and sprung rhythm, and forces the reader into reinterpreting his experience in the light of Christ by making equations out of seemingly disparate factors and by reconciling them through the use of language infused with Christian symbolism. As we have seen, Avison often utilizes dialectical structures in many of her poems in which the initial development, which introduces a theme, is followed by a caesura (visible or syntactical—usually both), the rest of the poem turning the initial meaning in on itself. Often puns are used to heighten this effect. But the end result is that the whole poem itself becomes one huge pun with the power to both de- and re-familiarize the reader. Poems are further destabilized by wordplay which may make of one word, such as "flies," or "still," a noun, a verb, a euphemism or an allusion. This jumbling of the senses is intrinsic to Avison's poetics: Avison's preoccupation with detail and her use of changing perspective combine to draw the reader both into and beyond the poems, enabling him to participate aesthetically in the Easter event—release from the death of winter, release from death-in-life—by making him feel that receiving the "implicit touch" is as "easy as breathing."

CHAPTER TWO

IN THE STRONG SUN

For now we see through a glass, darkly; but then
face to face: now I know in part; but then shall I
know even as also I am known
(1 Cor. 13:12).

"I want to be whole
never mind what it costs
anaesthesia, pill
skin-graft, cast—...."

        Oh, it cost.
        The whole
        Heart was glutted
        with us, turned inside out...

"Well, even that, if
therapies leave
nothing else I can try.
I want to be whole and okay before I die."

        In what glass
        do you look to assess
        this physique of yours?

the Book? or the people-pleaser's?

"What I expected was clearer
before you mentioned the mirror....
What time can I come back?
Next week?"

("The Evader's Meditation," *s*, 35)

The speaker in "The Evader's Meditation" is concerned with wholeness—at any "cost," unless, of course, there
is "nothing else [he] can try." The remedies he proposes are
the products of technology: "anaesthesia, pill / skin-graft,
cast" —"undeathful technicalities" (*s,* 11). The narrator
suggests, but never clearly defines, alternatives. These alternatives, however, have been clearly indicated in the first five
poems of this second section of *sunblue* whose main concern
is life "in the strong sun," a phrase which reflects Avison's
relational, rather than substantialist, ontology.
    As I mentioned in the introduction to this work, many
problems in understanding Avison's Christian vision stem
from the idea, Gnostic/Platonic in origin, that there is something inherently divine in man (*substantia*), which sets him
apart from all other creatures.[1] This is what is meant by a
substantialist ontology. Pushed to its extreme, this doctrine,
which speaks of "a merger of being, as in Neoplatonism,"
leads to pantheism.[2] In its more radical Christian forms, it has
led to a belief in the complete separation of the flesh and the
spirit, and to a theology which has tried to vindicate this
duality in man by subsuming it under the general category of
the war between the spirit and the flesh, leading in its turn to
the condemnation of physical desire.[3]
    A *relational ontology*, however, focuses on the "rela-
tionship between Creator and creature. The image of God is
something that 'happens' as a consequence of this relationship. The human creature images (used as a verb) its Creator
because and insofar as it is 'turned toward' God. To be *imago
Dei* does not mean to have something but to be and do
something: to image God."[4] The emphasis is clearly upon the

will. What is intended is "an alongsidedness, a vis-à-vis, a dialogue, a give and take, a back and forth."⁵ It is in this respect that Pauline theology, with it stress on a strong personal revelation and relationship, most differs from Johannine theology, where the emphasis is upon the sacramental, the mystical and the liturgical.

In both "Sounds Carry" (s, 30) and "Thirst" (s, 31) we are given a portrayal of wholeness, one that depends strongly on the contrast, or rather, contiguity of sacred and profane time. What is alluded to is "a sacramental unified field, as it were, in which Creation and Redemption are one act of will existing outside time—or, more exactly, at the intersection of time and eternity."⁶

In "Sounds Carry," the strong sun of "summer / undefines place," and yet is itself defined by a "nimbus," which highlights the sacral nature of the sun/Son. A similar paradox extends to the realm of time: yet here it is a defining of the undefinable that is occurring. The reader is next guided into the heart of the poem by Avison's close attention to detail, her landscape photographer's ability to play with depth of field: the "process of approaching awareness by moving through particulars."⁷ The poem moves from the invisible through the "hidden" and on to the obvious. By drawing on images previously used in *sunblue*, Avison allows for a larger repertoire upon which to work her strategies. One is reminded of the "dog," "mist" and "visual amplitude" in "SKETCH: From train window," the "robin's toe-pronging," in "Grass Roots" with its prophecies of summer ("Summer is so"), and the life "underfoot" of "SKETCH: End of day." There are, as well, the "flies," with all their nuances, of "SKETCH: A work gang," the "weathered door" of "SKETCH: A childhood place" (through the words "the / sun on worn boards") and the "easy as breathing" of "March Morning." One could go on. The point is that Avison is calling upon the experience of the reader of her poems, an experience fresh with images of release and redemption, and challenging it to grasp that into which it has been released. How *does* one speak about the ineffable? How does one understand "now"? What is it like to be in, "to wait / in, the strong sun"?

"Thirst" further whets the reader's appetite. Like the "flock" in "Person" (*WS/D*, 146) that is "drenched with Being," the "deer" of "Thirst" are "steeped" "beyond the rim of here." And yet, not quite, for Avison's metaphysical magic captures the deer between time and eternity through the subtle use of a syntax that leaves the reader with the image of the deer both "not yet / drinking" and "not yet . . . beyond the rim of here"! There is both a continuation and an amplification of the paradoxes in "Sounds Carry" which is further developed through a series of oxymorons that yoke movement with stillness, anticipation with release, and presence with absence. It is in this poem that Avison introduces the epistemological problem with which she deals throughout the volume: how is it that in the sacred presence—the "now," the "here" and the "still"—God, the "pure, onflowing," is still "not yet known"?[8] How do we know that we know? Avison suggests several possibilities. In "Listening" (*s*, 58) she says:

> Because I know
> the voice of the Word
> is to be heard
> I know I do not know . . .

While in "Oughtiness Ousted" (*s*, 64),

> God (being good) has let me know
> no good apart from Him,

and in "Contest" (*s*, 66), Avison propounds her Augustinian epistemology.[9]

> Having in Adam chosen to know
> we are sorely honoured in
> choosing to know, I know.
>
> We do know what we do.
> The second Adam chose to know but
> to do otherwise, thus condemning
> all but the goodness He
> thus declares knowable.

Grimly we concede it, who
would rather do and know,
until as we are known we know.

We are "not yet / drinking" because of our
"invented[ness]" (s, 64), because of our sin: Of course we
"want to be whole," but we are unwilling to pay the price, and
so settle for "undeathful technicalities, / hurt that they click"
(s, 11).

I think that one of the foremost problems confronting
the reader of Avison's Christian poetry is not the requirement
for "biblical literacy" on the part of the reader, as William
Aide seems to think,[10] but, rather, the lack of a sound knowledge of theology. One can cite, for example, Williamson's
unusual reading; or Klus's gnostic one—the result of Redekop's influence; or even St. Pierre's attempt to read Avison
in a manner analogous to the *Spiritual Exercises* of St.
Ignatius. Too much has been made of Avison's Johannine
affinities, based in part upon her salvation experience "while
reading the fourteenth chapter of John's Gospel,"[11] and in part
upon Redekop's insistence that "for her . . . the single most important chapter in the Bible is the first chapter of the Gospel
of John."[12] This insistence upon the word/Word relationship
has led Redekop into eisegesis—in other words "reading
into," instead of exegesis, which term is applied to the results
of a valid hermeneutical, or interpretive enterprise—as is
obvious in his attempt to use "The Bible to be Believed" to
prove his theories. While on one hand he himself admits that
"the tone of the second version of the poem, and indeed its
kerygmatic emphasis, are changed from the first by Avison's
removal of the penultimate stanza of the original, which
establishes a close personal relation between poet and Word/
word,"[13] he, nevertheless, tries to make of Christ (the Word)
something other than the second Person of the Trinity: "truly
God and truly man."[14] This is obvious, for instance, when
Redekop refers to Jesus' humanity as "temporary"[15] —a
blatant heresy for those who ascribe to the Nicene Creed, one
of the foundations of orthodoxy.[16] As Lawrence Mathews
points out, those who see "poetry [as] the supreme fiction of

which religion is a manifestation,"[17] will, of course, see "Jesus [as] the perfect Romantic artist whose poem is the world,"[18] and also believe that poets are

> the hierophants of an unapprehended inspiration, the mirrors of the gigantic shadows which futurity casts upon the present, the words which express what they understand not; the trumpets which sing to battle, and feel not what they inspire: the influence which is moved not, but moves; [that] poets are the unacknowledged legislators of the World.[19]

This association has a long pre-history and has continued right up into the present as the "pagan" alternative to orthodox Christianity.[20] This philosophy of "ontic union belongs to the tradition of Athens—to the mystery religions, for example, with their goal of incorporation into the deity and the consequent loss of self."[21] What Avison is pointing towards, however, is an "alongsidedness,"[22] albeit one based totally on faith, a faith based on the Bible to be believed, which as Redekop rightly points out is central to Avison's faith.

Avison's theology is *not* Johannine but Pauline: it is Christocentric, rather than Logocentric, stressing both Christ's humanity[23] and his divinity;[24] it stresses Christ's functional role as not only Savior-Redeemer[25] but also as "the meaning and goal of all creation."[26] It is Pauline theology which stresses that "Christians live in the *eschaton* . . . an age of dual polarity . . . an age that looks backward to the first Good Friday and Easter Sunday and forward to a final glorious consummation when 'we shall always be with the Lord.'"[27] This is the expectation both of the deer in "Thirst," captured between time and eternity, and of the narrator in "SKETCH: A childhood place." Other poems in *sunblue* which reflect Avison's strongly Pauline orientation are "He Couldn't be Safe," where Christ is the suffering servant of Isaiah 53:5; "The Circuit," where the glory of Christ is his obedience unto death and his vicarious atonement;[28] "The Bible to be Believed," where the "Word" is "the living Word," a human person, a boy, "a Jewish-Egyptian / firstborn," subject to human temptation, and, at the same time, *Kyrios*, "Lord"; "Listening," where the "Word" is the "Lord / who chose being born to die / and died to bring alive"; "Absolute," where Christ is a "Person"; "Until Christmas," where Jesus, the Word, is "helplessly human," speeding "towards the Cross"; "Christmas: Becoming," where Christ is "only son of man / torn and entombed, but raised / timeless"; and "Slow Advent," where Jesus is *not* "incarnate as reborn language,"[29] but is

> the flint-set-faced
> ready-for-gallows One,
> on, on, into glory, and His
> place of my being to be
> His as will every
> place
> be.

Moreover, Avison's frequent allusions to the Eucharist are also strongly Pauline. First, in that she sees the Eucharist as "a memorial and proclamation of Christ's sacrificial death, it is a rallying point: 'As often as you eat this bread and drink of this cup, you proclaim the death of the Lord, until he comes' (1 Cor. 11:26)"; and second, she proclaims the "eschatological aspect [of] the Eucharist: for the proclamation of that death must continue 'until he comes.' It is only Christ in his risen, glorious body who fully accomplishes the salvation of those who partake of the table of the *Kyrios*."[30]

The consequences of the "evader's" choice to try everything but "the Book" (*s*, 35), the Fall, are examined in "While as yet no leaves may fall" (*s*, 32), "Morning Bus" (*s*, 33) and "A Lament" (*s*, 34). In "While as yet no leaves may fall,"[31] death is not mentioned, as in the poem from which this line is taken; yet the reader has the unmistakable feeling that death is being spoken of in both of these poems.[32] This is suggested, in Avison's poem, by words such as "broken light," "distantly," "last / lucid wash of light," "motors sighed," "soughed," "chapel," "stiff," "old," "evening" and the 'weeping' "willows," symbols of mourning. Unlike Barnes' poem, however, the sense of expectation at the end of "A Lament" is much stronger as the poem ends with "the evening meadows wait[ing] under the willow trees."

Two curious images, "burbling" pigeons, and "sigh[ing]" motors, are repeated in "Morning Bus," —whose title contains an obvious pun on 'mourning'—in the "sigh[ing]" bus qua fish. We note the odd syntax that makes the lake breathe air filtered by the bus, and that inverts the natural order by presenting nature as dead (the "flattened" bird), and the machine as alive (the breathing "bus"). Something is "foul," "rancid," inescapably wrong, inescapably earthbound: "The feathers flutter / on unflyable wings."

It is not only the animal world, however, that is incapacitated but also the human:

> We breathe.
> We jolt. This slump of letting be
> refuses fusion; it is a
> non-homogeneity that goes on.
>
> For each, enough
> is destination.

In "A Lament" the images of death and decay from the previous two poems are brought together, and their cause is specified as the Fall, through the use of the word "fall," "fault," and the allusion to *Paradise Lost* Book 9, line 782, that fateful moment when Eve plucked the fruit from Eden's tree:

> What fear I then, rather what know to fear
> Under this ignorance of Good and Evil,
> Of God or Death, of Law or Penalty?
> Here grows the Cure of all, this Fruit Divine,
> Fair to the Eye, inviting to the Taste,
> Of virtue to make wise: what hinders then
> To reach, and feed at once both Body and Mind?
>   So saying, her rash hand in evil hour
> Forth reaching to the Fruit, she pluck'd she eat:
> Earth felt the wound, and Nature from her seat
> *Sighing* through all her Works gave signs of woe
> That all was lost [emphasis mine].[33]

46

The key word linking these poems is, of course, "sighing,"—skilfully left unsaid in "A Lament." Other linking devices are the references to birds, death, decay, "airflow" ("bus's gills"; "motors sighed"), and "meadows." We note the allusions to the "cyanide jar" of "Butterfly Bones OR Sonnet Against Sonnets" (*WS/D*, 29) in the words "Death has us glassed in," and other allusions to "signs of woe" which reinforce the sense of despair and entrapment of postlapsarian existence.

As we return to "The Evader's Meditation," then, it becomes obvious that the speaker's desire "to be whole," is the result not only of the Fall, but also of his own choice to find "the Cure of all," while claiming ignorance of God's will. The narrator in "The Evader's Meditation," who could quite well be the angel of "A Work-Up" (*s*, 37)—both poems have similar geographies and structures—draws upon the images of the first poems of this section of *sunblue* as well as upon Biblical references to remind the speaker of the "cost": "The whole / heart was glutted / with us, turned inside out..." recalls not only the "gizzard and some ruby parts,"—"the viscera"—of "A Lament," as well as the "bird flattened on the road's shoulder," of "Morning Bus," but also refers to Jesus' heart being pierced by the soldier's spear,[34] and to the fact that His death is a vicarious atonement for our disobedience.[35] Similarly the "glass" recalls both "death," which "has us glassed in," and the "jar" of "Butterfly Bones." But "glass," here, has another connotation: a "mirror," the soul of man.[36] The advice of the narrator to the evader is that he take God's Word seriously to heart, and also have a good look at himself; the evader, like Eve, balks, expecting the mirror to be "clearer"— one notes the pun. There are, however, no easy solutions, no discounts, for believer and unbeliever alike: "we see through a glass darkly," says St. Paul, indicating that "all earthly knowledge is partial"; that "while we live out our lives on this earth our sight of things eternal is, at best, indistinct."[37] The speaker must make a choice between the "cyanide jar [that] seals life" and life "beyond the rim of here"; between settling for a destination that is "enough" ("Morning Bus," *s*, 33), and going on: "There is a direction [!] And it's *on* [!]" ("On?", *s*, 36).

One of the major ramifications of Avison's Pauline theology has been her preoccupation with life in the here-and-now. This has manifested itself in a commitment to service in her daily life,[38] and to the propagation of a social gospel in her poetry.

Two of Avison's key strategies in proclaiming this kerygma are her use of language, and her use of design on the page. Through both of these techniques, she is able to engage the reader, de-familiarize him, and draw him into new possibilities of meaning.

> One looks about at the green-hung room of this earth
> as though as seed in the soil
> still, and about to split
> rotting with reaches towards the
> inconceivable elsewhere,
>
> knowing no purposing, only
> a kind of atavistic feelers-out,
> as a comber shells,
> arched, day after day, to
> shatter waveness.
>
> Nevertheless
> becomings are then in now;
> unbearable unless suffered:
>
> hope stirs,
> not surges.

"As Though" (*s*, 70) is a perfect example of how Avison uses arrangement on the page and rhetorical devices to lead the reader into the space beyond the text.[39] The typography suggests the shape of a funnel; however, because the last two lines are equal in length there is a sense of finality which conflicts with the idea of movement as expressed within the last stanza, and conveyed by the uneven word lengths. The physical geography of the poem thus acts out the fact that "hope stirs" at the end of the poem. The crammed and irregular pentameter of the first line reflects the density of the "green-hung . . . earth," while the antanaclasis on "as" has a paradoxical effect, since this line, which has an underlying smoothness because of the assonance on the sibilants, jolts the reader with its shifts in emphasis and subsequent ambiguity: to what exactly does "the seed in the soil" refer? To the "room," or to the persona of the poem? Enjambment between "soil" and "still," "split" and "rotting," and "the" and "inconceivable" continues the tension and ambiguity throughout the stanza as does the antanaclasis on "still" (adjective, adverb) and "reaches" (noun, verb). Note, also, how the sense of "reaching towards" is conveyed through both the visual and the syntactical: the fourth line of the first stanza juts beyond its neighbours—as does "feelers-out" in the second stanza—and creates suspense through the separation of the article from its substantive. The reader is confused: Is the reaching out "towards the inconceivable" or towards an "inconceivable elsewhere": the former defines an undefinable place, while the latter "undefines place" ("Sounds Carry," *s*, 30). We remember that this idea was used to great effect in "Thirst" and "Sounds Carry," where Avison plays with concepts of time and place.

Paronomasia (punning) on "knowing" and "no" emphasizes the epistemological theme of this poem, as do "*nev*ertheless" and "*un*less," and "*un*bearable *un*less." The use of antitheses, both explicit ("then and now") and implicit ("hope stirs, / not"), and the use of repetition ("*un*bearable *un*less") amplify this sense of tense stasis in the poem. The tedium of "day after day" is in opposition to the movement of the waves—a movement which is neither forward ("becomings are then in now"), nor backward ("atavistic"). "One" is left only with possibilities, a great verbal *as though*. As Willmot points out, "In 'As Though' . . . faith is seen as a form of gradual self-destruction, like the 'rotting with reaches' of a seed. Through that unoptimism, the poem unfolds organically towards a tiny, cotyledon-like affirmation. It is formally and rhetorically perfect."[40]

"From a Public Library Window" (*s*, 62) is another poem where Avison's use of language and design on the page lead the reader into the unexpected.

> The uncoiling, jointed, glass-and-duragloss-
> plated, flowing
> serpent of traffic will
> be stilled.

> The seemingly stilled, upthrust
> office and apartment towers
> and smokestacks
> will with the slow
> of brickdust-Nineveh's flow,
> (and even the basking hills)
> sift down and be all through.

> The tissue moon still floating in skylake
> and the sunflooding sunfire point—
>   swivel of food and drink and sense—
> from before Adam, wait
> for the once opening of
> the Golden Gate.

> Only the unchanging One
> is, inexhaustibly, un-done.

The run-on line, compound epithet, and run-on sentence structure of the first stanza create the sensation of a serpent "uncoiling," a movement which is maintained through the run-on sentence structure of the following two stanzas. The rhyme on "will" and "still" is onomatopoeic, bringing the flow almost to a halt; but this is undone in the following line through the sound and sense of "seemingly stilled" where long vowels, liquids and sibilants revive the flowing movement of the poem.

In the first stanza the adjective "stilled" refers to a future action; in the second the action is conditional; and in the third stanza "still" is both adverb and noun, but the activity described is in the present. Other devices used are paradox ("jointed" "serpent"), polyptoton ("glass," "duragloss";

"stilled," "still"; "once," "Only," "One"), repetition ("will," "stilled"), kennings ("skylake," "sunflooding sunfire point"), and antanaclasis ("even" as verb/adverb, and "un-done").

The poetic strategies enable the reader to participate in the sense of futility which results from man's inability to accept his mortality. The poem, although forever "uncoiling," is never "undone," while mankind, seeking to outdo nature, shall, like "Nineveh," pass away:

> We are forever
> doing, done to.

> The grass grows
> strongly, it has twitchgrass in
> it too, ready even
> to shag the tracks and blocks
> if we fall
> silent or
> simply let be.
> ("Transients," *s*, 82)

"Scar-face" (*s*, 72) is one of Avison's more remarkable poems in that it confronts the reader with an issue with which most of us would rather not deal. The "social gospel" propounded in "Scar-face," "Needy," "We the Poor who are Always with us," "We are not Poor, not Rich," and "To a Pioneer in Canadian Studies; And to all in such Pedantry," reflects Avison's relational, rather than substantialist, ontology, her Pauline-Christian concern for the quality of life "in the strong sun."

> Scarred—beyond what plastic surgery
> could do, or where
> no surgeon was when blasted
> in the wilds or
> > on a sideroad—

> he prows his life through
> the street's flow and wash

51

of other's looks.

His face is a good
face, looking-out-from.

One of the main techniques used in "Scar-face" is the
recalling of images from earlier poems in *sunblue*, as well as
a reference from Souster's "Roller Skate Man."[41] "Plastic sur-
gery" recalls the "skin-graft" and the theme, in general, of
"The Evader's Meditation" (*s*, 35) (wholeness and its cost),
while "blasted / in the wilds or / on a sideroad" recalls both the
"gizzard and some ruby inner parts" of "A Lament" (*s*, 34),
and the "bird . . . flattened on the road's shoulder" in "Morning
Bus" (*s*, 33). "The street's flow and wash" is, of course, a
variation upon Souster's "flotsam among the jetsam of your
world."

In the first stanza the reader is given a description of a
"scarred" or otherwise physically mutilated figure. Because
of associations established previously, the reader may be led
to expect that this figure is most probably the wild creature of
" A Lament," or "Morning Bus " However, in the second
stanza, the reader's expectations are thwarted. By identifying
the "scarred" figure as a "he," Avison forces an identification
with the subject, and, thus, evokes feelings of empathy from
the reader. A new set of associations is now called into play,
those from "The Evader's Meditation" and also those from
poems which deal with human violence in *sunblue*: "A Blurt
on Gray" (*s*, 85) and "Embattled Deliverance" (*s*, 87). The
reader may be led to feel that he can understand the disfigure-
ment of another as long as it may be accidental, or if it is
associated with a "noble" cause, such as war. Again, images
may be recalled of the transients of "SKETCH: A work gang
on Sherbourne" (*s*, 12), an association reinforced by the implicit reference to Souster's poem. One may conjure up
images of an old, war veteran who has fallen upon hard times,
and yet, can be pitied, accepted, because we have a social slot
for his type.

But the last stanza of the poem destroys any vestige of
these self-aggrandizing rationalizations. "His face," we are

told, "is a good/ face." By breaking the line after "good" Avison causes the reader to pause on this word and bring out its associations. The subject of the poem *is* "good." Moreover, his face is not scarred: it "is a good / face." At this point the reader is confronted with a gap in his understanding which is caused by this shifting of theme and horizon. At this point also, the reader may be lead to fill in this blank by asking why, if it is a "good / face," he has been under the impression that it is not, and why he has been under the impression that the subject is seriously disfigured.

The answer is that the "face is a good / face, looking-out-from," the subject does not see himself as being disfigured in any way, and it is society's judgement that has branded this individual as "scarred." The "beyond" of the first stanza now becomes an "inside," while the "others' looks" become yours and mine. Of course, there is always the possibility that the reader himself may be the subject, since it is he who is "looking-out-from" during the act of reading. Is it the reader who is "scarred"? Who, exactly, is in need?

A) In part, who isn't
      miserly with his need—
      or needled by it—
      or debonair
      as though it were not there—
      or, at best, genuinely free
          to need yet never be
          needy?

B) "The poor are always being
   inspected: by the
      Fire Department, for litter, oily rags, those
      lamp-cords from the washing-machine to
      the hall ceiling socket, etc.;
         by the
      'worker' with new forms
      to be written on;
         by the
      mission visitor 'to invite
      you to the children's pageant';

somebody even inspects
to check on whether it's true you keep chickens and goats!"

C) Home after a day of calls
she absent-mindedly pulls
the curtains first
and then acknowledges a thirst:
everything has run out
again tonight.

("Needy," s, 78)

  Ostensibly simple, "Needy" is another Avisonian tour
de force, its rhetorical devices destabilizing the text suffi-
ciently that the reader cannot help but be drawn in. The poem
is composed of three vignettes, each quite independent of the
others. In the first, a rhythm is established through polyptoton
("need," "needled" and "needy"), anaphora ("or"), and end-
rhyme, with the pun on "free" and "be" — freebie. Various
postures are proposed vis-à-vis "need" which are suggestive
of the performance rhetoric of the "prospector"-professor of
"To a Pioneer in Canadian Studies; And to all in such Pedantry" (*s*, 83), and his ilk in "Us Artists—Before Public was,
or Grants: OR, Can Litter" (*s*, 42). Sandwiched between the
essential question—"In part, who isn't . . . needy?"—is a
diatribe of narcissistic proportions, designed for "preserving"
(*s*, 83), not finding.

  The second vignette of "Needy" comprises a quota-
tion, epistolary in tone (not form), which, through the words
"poor" and *"always,"* and because it is opposite the poem "We
the *Poor* who are *Always* with us" (*s*, 79), recalls Mark 14:7:
"For ye have the *poor* with you *always*, and whensoever ye
will ye may do them good: but me ye have not *always*." In fact
it is through the words *"poor"* and *"always"* and Mark 14:7
that "Needy," "We the Poor who are Always with us" and "We
are not Poor, not Rich" (*s*, 81) are linked.

  Apparently not even the religious are spared as the
"mission visitor" is relegated to "'worker' with new forms,"
and the poor are turned into statistics. But in the third vignette
the theme shifts, forcing the reader to make sense of this new

horizon: Who is "she"? Why is "she" "pull[ing] the curtains"? What is her "thirst"? Of what nature were her "calls"? What is the "everything [that] has run out"?

"She" may be one of the "needy" who has been out all day looking for work ("after a day of calls") and who comes home in defeat to an impoverished existence. But I think "she" is the "mission visitor" of the second vignette—in this case the poem may be autobiographical, especially if we consider those poems which satirize or otherwise reject the academic life to be autobiographical statements as well—and her "thirst" is for spiritual strength, since she is emotionally spent, much as the narrator in "Searching and Sounding," who finds Christ

> in the sour air
> of a morning-after rooming-house hall-bedroom;
> not in Gethsemane's grass, perfumed with prayer,
> but here,
> seeking to cool the grey-stubbled cheek
>   and the filth-choked throat
>   and the scalding self-loathing heart, and
> failing . . . .

(WS/D, 154)

Why does she "try on and on, still?" (*s*, 79). We note the three capitalized words of "*We* the *Poor* who are *Always* with us," and the message this conveys. If "we" are "always" "poor," what is the point of trying, of going on? After all, the "hungry" are a burden ("cumbering") and the "ill" "uncaring." And no matter what our good intentions, the situation just doesn't seem to change. Perhaps the problem is that our endeavour is predicated upon our volition: that we "try *as* we will"; that we "try on and on, *still?*" that is, in a state of stasis.

The second stanza of "We the Poor who are Always with us" contains some specific Biblical allusions which may help to shed some light on the problem of going on in the face of insurmountable despair:

> Try on and on, still?
> In fury, fly

out, smash shards? (And quail
at tomorrow's new supply,
and fail anew to find and smash the why?)

The words "shards" and "quail / at tomorrow's new supply"
draw upon Romans 9: 18-22, Jeremiah 18:1-6, 2 Corinthians
4:7, Exodus 16: 12-15 and John 6: 31-32, 48-51, all of which
speak about the unmerited grace of God and His revelation in
His son Jesus.

    The giving of the manna and the quail[42] was God's
reaction to the murmuring of Israel in the wilderness (we note
the murmuring of the narrator in the second and third stanzas
of "We the Poor who are Always with us"), and is interpreted
by Christians as a type of both Christ and the Eucharist.[43] The
"shards" refer both to God as the "potter" and also to the fact
that any good we do comes of God: for we "have this treasure
in earthen vessels, that the excellency of the power may be of
God, and not of us."[44] That humanity apparently has no say in
the matter causes our egos to "in fury, fly / out, smash shards,"
and to "try to smash the why."[45]   Yet man forgets one
important thing: that it is the potter who has power over the
clay, who

    willing to shew his wrath, and to make his power
    known, endured with much longsuffering the
    vessels of wrath fitted to destruction: And that he
    might make known the riches of his glory on the
    vessels of mercy , which he had afore prepared
    unto glory.[46]

Thus the reference to "shards" is two-edged: on one hand, it
alludes to God's righteous judgement in the *eschaton*; on the
other, it deals with the difficult nature of the spiritual path in
the present—the "soppy sand" of "this Despond" (*s*, 81),
wherein, at most, we may try

    to learn to expect to
    pour it out

into desert—to find out what it is.

(*s*, 50)

In the third stanza of "We the Poor who are Always with us," paronomasia on "too" (adverb/preposition), antanaclasis on "still" (adjective / verb), and paradox ("free to love / past use, where none survive") combine to deform the text and prompt the reader into action, forcing him to "ideate the hidden cause of the apparent deformations."[47] What *is* this poem pointing towards? Avison, however, does provide us with clues in the words "there" (twice as adverb / noun) and "then": "there" as noun refers to heaven, where "reason" (logos) awaits that day, "then," when man as we know him shall be no more and God will be all in all. We who are neither "poor" nor "rich," like "Rita" and "Vivian," or Mary and Martha,[48] can only "hope" that "in the strong sun"

Speeding by the unmoving is
for each alike a known
blessedness not our own.
And each, in that, goes on.

(*s*, 81)

CHAPTER THREE

RESTORATION

And I saw a new heaven and a new earth: for the
first heaven and the first earth were passed away;
and there was no more sea.
     And I saw no temple therein: for the
Lord God Almighty and the Lamb are the temple
of it. And the city had no need of the sun, neither
of the moon, to shine in it: for the glory of God
did lighten it, and the Lamb is the light thereof
(Rev. 21:1, 22-23).

The leopard and the kid
     are smoothness (fierce)
     and softness (gentle)
       and will lie down together.
Then, storm and salt and largeness, known, in time,
       will be within the wholely pure,
          the unimaginable!

     Then, the fair blue
     will not be star-extinguishing;
     and one cascading meadowlark
     an all-where will not deafen;
     acute, prefiguring moments
     of our leaf-flickered day
       will lose none of their poignancy

> when they are caught up, Then, in the
> all-things-upgathering bliss.
>
> Here, then, prophetically,
> in the strange peace of the outcast
> on manger hay
> lies a real baby:
>
> > all-cherishing, the unsourced,
> > the never fully celebrated
> > well-spring of That Day.
>
> ("Then," *s*, 98)

As Alan Watts correctly points out, "Christianity is an eschatological, not a historical, religion—for its whole hope is directed towards *Dies illa*, 'that Day,' upon which time and history will come to an end."[1] Which, of course, means that for the Christian this world will always be imperfect: true restoration cannot occur here, but only in a "new heaven and a new earth."[2]

The poems in *sunblue* have preoccupied themselves, as we have seen, with

> ...... a time
> of bony men and doom
> lit towards the bread and drink of Him
> whose is the final kingdom;
>
> ("Dryness and Scorch of
> Ahab's Evil Rule," *s*, 51)

they have concerned themselves with the paradox of life both consciously within, or oblivious to, God's Grace:

> The sun burns down on all
> who linger and who go,
>
> ("Into the Vineyard:
> a Vision," *s*, 67)

and

        the Pure can bless
        on earth *and* from on high
        ineradicably

                                              ("Light (III)," *s*, 61)

and they have suggested that despite our technological ad-
vances ("we float, not 'fly', / keeping check on the fading air
and power / supply) (*s*, 89) our progress is merely self-
deception—true meaning "will be given only to / recovered
innocence." We must be "content to wait till Then" (*s*, 75).
    Because "time / will be within the wholely pure" in
Dies illa the

        acute, prefiguring moments
        of our leaf-flickering day
        will lose none of their poignancy.

                                                         (*s*, 98)

Time, itself, shall be no more.[3] But what shall be (or not be)
in *Dies illa* depends on what happened in *illo tempore*:
"then."[4] And what happens "here" (which is "then, prophetically") determines what shall happen "then," in the future
(*Dies illa*). Avison makes it clear that all of this wonderfully
convoluted metaphysics is actually quite simple: It depends
not upon some abstract principle, but upon "One Person," (*s*,
86) who, *in time*, became

                a real baby:

                        all-cherishing, the unsourced,
                        the never fully celebrated
                        well-spring of That Day

                                              ("Then," *s*, 98)

Although "Christianity is an eschatological, not a historical,
religion," Christianity's eschatology is based upon history,

upon the fact that God works within a linear and not a mythical (circular/ cyclical) historical framework.[5] This theme is one about which Avison is particularly emphatic. For Avison Jesus is not an idea, nor is the Bible a book of myths. The truths of the Bible are as applicable today as they were "then":

> The Word alive cherishes all:
> doves, lambs—or whale—
> beyond old rites or emblem burial.
> Grapes, bread, and fragrant oil:
> all that means, is real
> now, only as One wills.
>
> ("The Bible to be Believed," *s*, 56)

The irony of it all, especially for the artist who is continually concerned with the nature of his/her art, is not only that you can't take it with you, but that nothing was ever really made—only rearranged:

> The evasive "maker"-metaphor,
> thank God, under the power
> of our real common lot
> leads stumbling back to what it promised to evade.
> There is no one reviewed, no viewer,
> no one of us not creature;
> we're apparently at work. But nothing is made
> except by the only unpretentious, Jesus Christ, the /
> Lord.
>
> ("Creative Hour," *s*, 99)

This distinction between the Creator and the creature is the distinguishing mark between Christian theology and Hellenistic philosophy,[6] and, as indicated above, is what distances Avison's poetics from any vestiges of romanticism.

In "Creative Hour" other foreshadowings of the *eschaton* are alluded to: the periphlegethon[7] at the end of time (the destruction of the earth by fire), and the resurrection.

> The outlines vanish.
> The tentative image fails.
> Chalks smear, all the paint spills,
> creation crumples and curls.
>
> I'm down to bone and awe.
> Where is this then—
> no clock, no lunch, no law?

Truly what is being spoken of here is anagogic "jail-break /
[a]nd re-creation" (*WS/D*, 27): "What is learned, I unlearn."
    Nowhere is the paradox of faith more eloquently
expressed than in "Light (I)":

> The stuff of flesh and bone
> is given, *datum*. Down
> the stick-men, plastiscene-
> people, clay-lump children, are strewn,
> each casting shadow in the eye of day.
>
> Then—listen!—I see
> breath of delighting rise from
> those stones the sun touches
> and hear a snarl of breath
> as mouth sucks air. And with
> shivery sighings—see: they stir
> and turn and move, and power
> to build, to undermine, is theirs,
> is ours.
>
> The stuff, the breath, the power to move even thumbs
> and with them, things: *data*. What is
> the harpsweep on the heart for?
> What does the constructed power
> of speculation reach for?
> Each of us casts a shadow in the bewildering day,
>   an own-shaped shadow only.

The light has looked on Light.

He from elsewhere
speaks; he breathes impasse-
crumpled hope even
in us:
that near.

(s, 59)

This poem reads like a compendium of the cultural history of the Western world. It ranges from philosophical arguments about the nature of matter (*substantia*), that is "stuff," through to what appears to be a Democritan metaphysics ("Down"; "strewn") and on to empiricism and logical positivism ("*datum*"). It builds upon the etiological myth of Pyrrha and Deucalion,[8] relies upon anthropology in distinguishing man from the lower primates ("even thumbs"), refers to the poetic idea of the human soul as an aeolian harp (see above), and makes passing comment on the self-enterprising spirit of mankind at Babel:

> . . . power
> to build, to undermine, is theirs,
> is ours.

All of this happens/happened "Then"—that mythical time, both historically and existentially, before "the light has looked on Light." Just as each "here" is a "then, prophetically," both past and present, so the re-creation and restoration of life is possible when we possess that "crumpled hope"; when "enough / is [*not*] destination" (*s*, 33) because we "know / the voice" (*s*, 58).[9]

Of note is the fact that Avison closes this volume as she began it: with SKETCH poems. Of interest is the fact that the last poem, although a SKETCH poem, is not labelled as such.[10] In any case, functionally, "Bereaved" serves as an epilogue to this volume:

The children's voices
all red and blue and green in the
queer April dimness—
just as Ur, at dusk, under the walls—

are a barbarous tongue, lost on
that unmirroring, immured,
that thumping thing,
the heavy adult heart.

The children's voices are
the immemorial chorus.

(*s*, 105)

To begin with, the title of this poem is rather enigmatic and immediately sets the reader off balance. Who, exactly, is bereaved, and why? The reader may note, after a cursory reading, that the answer is not quick in coming, and may, like Merrett, jump at interpretations which both this poem and Avison's poetic will not support. To make the claim that the children "embody the truth of the Tower of Babel" is Antichristian, and as such cannot be considered as a viable interpretation.[11] Rather, as bpNichol points out, the reader "can see here that whole notion that knowledge is always beginning anew, that we exist not in a state of knowing but in a state of not knowing, that we are constantly being born again into the world not knowing."[12]

Formally, "Bereaved" employs several rhetorical devices to convey its intentions. We note the repetition in line 1 and line 9 ("the children's voices") and the tension this creates; polysyndeton in the second line and asyndeton in the fourth bring out the "queer[ness]" of the line in between, a line left hanging both visually and grammatically (anacoluthon); anaphora on lines 6 and 7 ("that"), assonance ("unmirroring, immured"), alliteration ("that thumping thing"), and onomatopoeia ("the heavy adult heart") are also used.

As she has done elsewhere in *sunblue*, Avison utilizes a dialectical structure in this poem in which the preliminary development ("The children's voices") is followed by a caesura which acts as a commentary upon the initial thought: "The children's voices are / the immemorial chorus."

The commentary on the poem (the gloss, as it were) contains two levels of reference: the first is to the Ziggurat at Ur, the "red and blue and green" referring to the colourful temple atop the structure which contained an image of the god;[13] the second is to "Ur of the Chaldees" whence Abraham as a child, having glimpsed the gate, having known the voice of the true God, set off for the promised land.[14] The message of "Bereaved" thus not only echoes a theme that has run throughout this volume, but brings it full circle: in this life of "faithful unpredictability" (*s*, 104), where all are "child and forebear... together" (*s*, 101), one must "look to the sunblue" (*s*, 60) and live as though That Day were now.

Through her strategies of shifting theme and horizon whereby the de- and re-familiarization of the reader takes place, the skilful use of rhetorical devices which destabilize the text through the exploitation of linguistic possibilities, and the use of a repertoire rich in both biblical and theological allusions, Avison has shown the reader that there does indeed live a "dearest freshness deep down things," and that "the world is charged with the grandeur of God."[15] But she has also shown him that this world, although it is *sunblue*, is also full of other things: pollution, pain, isolation, doubt, hunger, thirst, loneliness and death.

Since her first volume of poems, *Winter Sun*, which is punctuated by existential despair, and where man is often portrayed as nothing more than "packaged us-es" (*WS/D*, 55)—

I lived towards the mortal Friday for-
                              ever till caught
                              in this

                                        (*s*, 94)

Avison has come to a rich and powerful understanding of both the Gospel and her role as a Christian poet. In her unambiguous proclamation of the orthodox faith she has turned neither to the right nor to the left, but, instead, has followed the straight and narrow of both her spiritual and artistic intentions. As she points out in "Strong Yellow, for Reading Aloud":

Who I was then we
both approach timorously—
or I do, believe me!
But I think, reading the lines,
the person looking *up* like that
was all squeezed solid, only a crowd-pressed
mass of herself at shoulder-
level, as it were, or at least
nine to noon, and the p.m. still to come
day *in* day *out* as the saying goes
which pretty well covers everything
or seems to, in *and* out then,
        when it's like that: no heart, no surprises, no
people-scope, no utterances,
no strangeness, no nougat of delight
           to touch, and worse,
no secret cherished in the
midriff then.
Whom you look up from that to
is Possibility not
God.
    I'd think . . .

(*s,* 41)

For Avison, the restoration, like the resurrection, exists both in history and in *illo tempore*: Salvation is a continuous and timeless process, and life "in the strong sun," is infused with the sacramental presence of God. For Avison, the believer is already seated in heavenly places.[16] She knows, despite, at times, appearances to the contrary, that nothing can separate her from the love of God[17] because

then

. . . .

is still the Christmas presence,
flower-frail, approachable:
the timeless Father does not leave
us broken, in our trouble.

Even cited, at sea, shop-bound,
the *here* is veined
in light.

("Christmas Becoming,"*s*, 94)

Although Avison may be clear about what has tran-
spired in her life and its effect on her poetry, the transforma-
tion has caused a schism between her and many of her readers.
As David Kent points out,

> The rather muted response to *sunblue* tends to
> confirm what the reaction of Harrison and a few
> others hinted at: that Avison's sudden conversion
> to Christianity in 1963 and her commitment to
> being a Christian artist (with all that that entails)
> have effectively divided her audience into those
> readers who accept her stance and those who
> regard this commitment as damaging to her art,
> turning it into dogma and ideology.[18]

But it is not as though Avison herself were unaware of
the barriers facing the Christian writer. As she says,

> The professing Christian and the declared agnostic
> seem to be talking about the same thing. But there
> is an absolute, inevitable intolerance, on each side,
> of the other. Both seem to listen and to meet what
> is said, but each misconstrues what is heard, and
> speaks to a different issue.[19]

In "Muse of Danger," Avison considers the "all that
that entails": the relationship between the Christian poet and
his art. She points out that Christians, and not just non-
Christians, can be seriously misled as to the nature of the

relationship between the Holy Spirit and the muse. In discussing the ambiguity of terms such as "Christian poem," "Christian literature," or "Christian art," Avison notes that these terms imply (for the Christian) that

> good subject matter will ensure good art, or that a
> dedicated Christian who writes will by virtue of
> his dedication understand the art of writing well.
> But it is the word of God alone, the being of God
> alone, that is good without any admixture—light
> without any shadow of darkness at all.[20]

Holding to the above can lead to "acute conflict" in the Christian writer, while seeking safety in doctrinal purity can crush the poetic muse. Her conclusion is that the poet can never be safe.

Interestingly, Avison locates one of the sources of conflict in the writer in the contiguity of sacred and profane time. The Christian believes that he lives in two time fields, the mortal and the eternal, by virtue of his being "born again." He is, like the deer in "Thirst," "not yet / drinking"; yet he is "steeped" in the presence of God (s, 31). Thus for the Christian, the act of poetry—as well as all other acts other than worship—occurs in mortal time.[21]

Avison feels very strongly that the Christian is a witness above all else, as is witnessed in her own commitment to sharing the Gospel not only amongst the poor and downtrodden in Canada and abroad, but also to the spiritually undernourished who congregate in the halls of academe: "In His strange and marvellous mercy, God nonetheless lets the believer take a necessary place as a living witness, in behaviour with family and classmate and stranger, in conversation, or in a poem."[22]

She does not believe in "'preferred' subjects for Christians," but she feels that "writers can find opportunities to use literature to deepen human awareness."[23] Although Avison holds to an orthodox faith, she does not share in the pusillanimity often ascribed by unbelievers to those of an evangelical persuasion, and as pointed out above, any criticisms to this effect about her poetry are quite unfounded.[24]

Speaking about the relationship between words and experience for the Christian writer, Avison says:

> Most writers discover for themselves the distinction between devotional reality and literature. The experience of beauty is not alien to the worshipper's awareness of God (although it is possible for beauty to be cold, and cruel, and arrogant). . . .
>
> The Christian writer should remind himself to give careful scrutiny to any poems written out of such experiences [prayer] before making them public. And he should accept poetic impulse from every area of experience, and avoid looking for his "inspiration" only from the moments least accessible to lisping human terms.[25]

Lest any doubting Thomases remain, Avison expressly states her belief, as a poet and as a Christian, that "the culturally excellent is not necessarily the spiritually valid." Just as the Christian poet must exercise freedom from dogmatic restraint, he should also realize that "the known, already recognized means of ordering words in poems are not necessarily better than other means that may still be discovered."[26]

Margaret Avison certainly walks a tightrope, writing about a God in whom most modern men can no longer believe, in a language which most believers cannot understand. That Avison shall not be consigned to the dustheap of literary history is made certain not by the eternal nature of her subject matter but by her ability to make the reader feel and see and hear. In that she is able to lead the reader into the text, there is also the possibility that she can lead him beyond it. On her part, she has the requisite skill; one wonders if the reader has sufficient faith.

NOTES

Introduction—(pages 7-19)

1. For a complete listing of the works of Margaret Avison, see Francis Mansbridge, "Margaret Avison: An Annotated Bibliography," *The Annotated Bibliography of Canada's Major Authors,* ed. Robert Lecker and Jack David, 6 vols. (Toronto: ECW Press, 1985), 6: 13-66.

2. Saul Bellow. "The Gonzaga Manuscripts," *Contemporary American Short Stories,* ed. Douglas Angus and Sylvia Angus (New York: Fawcett Premier, 1967), 398.

3. See my article, "Through the Son: An Explication of Margaret Avison's 'Person'," *Canadian Poetry, Studies, Documents, Reviews* 22 (Spring-Summer, 1988), 40.

4. For an interesting and informative study of the use of allusions to the Bible in Avison's earlier work, see "Appendix 2" in Ernest Redekop's "The Word/word in Avison's Poetry," *"Lighting up the terrain" : The Poetry of Margaret Avison,* ed. David Kent (Toronto: ECW Press, 1987).

5. Ken Norris, *The Little Magazine in Canada 1925-80* (Toronto: ECW Press, 1984), 104.

6. See Ernest Redekop, "sun/Son light/Light: Avison's elemental *Sunblue," Canadian Poetry Studies, Documents, Reviews* 7 (1980): 21-37, and David Kent, ed., *"Lighting up the terrain" : The Poetry of Margaret Avison* (Toronto: ECW Press, 1987).

7. James Merrett, "The Ominous Centre: The Theological Impulse in Margaret Avison's Poetry," *White Pelican* 5.2 (1976), 14.

8. Martin Turnell, *Modern Literature and Christian Faith* (Westminster, Md.: Newman Press), 1.

9. *Ibid.*, 19
.
10. Ronald S. Wallace, "Sacrament," *The New International Dictionary of the Christian Church,* ed. J.D. Douglas (Grand Rapids: Zondervan, 1974), 871. See also Douglas John Hall, *Imaging God: Dominion as Stewardship* (Grand Rapids: Eerdmans, 1986).

11. George Johnston, "Avison's Temple," rev. of *sunblue*, by Margaret Avison, *Canadian Forum*, May 1979, 31.

12. Avison both uses and alludes to the colour green quite frequently, the colour of spiritual regeneration and restoration. We note that the colour green is composed of yellow (revealed truth, divinity, the presence of God i.e., sun/Son) and blue (heavenly love, Grace). Hence the title, *sunblue*. See George Ferguson, *Signs & Symbols in Christian Art* (London: Oxford UP, 1961).

13. William Aide, "An Immense Answering of Human Skies: The Poetry of Margaret Avison," *The Human Elements*, 2nd series, ed. David Helwig (Toronto: Oberon Press, 1981), 69.

14. G. Geddes, and Phyllis Bruce, eds., "Notes on the Poets," *15 Canadian Poets* (Toronto: Oxford UP, 1970), 267.

15. J. M. Kertzer, "Margaret Avison: Power, Knowledge and the Language of Poetry," *Canadian Poetry: Studies, Documents, Reviews* 4 (Spring-Summer 1979), 29-44.

16. W.H. New, "The Mind's Eyes (I's) (Ice): The Poetry of Margaret Avison," *Articulating West: Essays on Purpose and Form in Modern Canadian Literature,* by New (Toronto:

New Press, 1972), 234-258; and Ernest Redekop, *Margaret Avison,* Studies in Canadian Literature 9 (Toronto: Copp Clark, 1970).

17. Malcolm Ross, "The Writer as Christian," *The New Orpheus: Essays toward a Christian Poetic,* ed. Nathan A. Scott Jr. (New York: Sheed and Ward, 1964), 91.

18. Psalm 23; Revelation 21:5.

19. Wolfgang Iser, *The Act of Reading: A Theory of Aesthetic Response* (Baltimore: John Hopkins UP, 1978), 69. "The *conventions* necessary for the establishment of a situation might more fittingly be called the repertoire of the text. The *accepted procedures* we shall call the strategies, and the reader's participation will henceforth be referred to as the realization."

20. *Ibid.,* 35-38, 163-167.

21. Robert C. Newman, "Natural Theology," *The New International Dictionary of the Christian Church,* ed. J.D. Douglas et al. (Grand Rapids: Zondervan, 1974), 695.

22. J. M. Kertzer, "Margaret Avison: Power, Knowledge and the Language of Poetry," *Canadian Poetry: Studies, Documents, Reviews* 4 (Spring-Summer 1979).

23. Terence Hawkes, *Structuralism and Semiotics* (Berkeley, Ca.: U of California P, 1977), 66.

24. *Ibid.,* 103.

25. *Religion and Art.* The Aquinas Lecture, 1963 (Milwaukee: Marquette UP, 1963), 20.

26. E.D. Hirsch Jr. *Validity in Interpretation* (New Haven: Yale UP), 5.

27. Christopher Klus, "The Religious Poetry of Margaret Avison," unpublished M.A. thesis, McMaster University, 1972, 8.

28. Jeannette St. Pierre, "Avison and the Metaphysicals," unpublished M.A. thesis, McMaster University, 1982, 93.

29. *Ibid.*, 94. Personal communication from Margaret Avison.

30. Lawrence M. Jones, "A Core of Brilliance: Margaret Avison's Achievement," *Canadian Literature* 38 (Autumn 1968), 51. See also my article on "Person" where I make a similar claim.

31. Redekop, "sun/Son," 25; Paul McNally, rev. of *sunblue*, by Margaret Avison, *The Fiddlehead* 123 (Fall 1979), 101.

Chapter One *Release*—(pages 20-38)

1. Albert Moritz, "Stalking the Sacred Asparagus," rev. of *sunblue*, by Margaret Avison, *Books in Canada* Aug.-Sept. 1979, 29-30. Moritz thinks otherwise. He says that although "Avison's faith is expressed in natural images and thus implies the salvation of the natural world . . . in fact her language has become allegorical," 29. This is not accurate; the roots of such an argument lie in a tradition which would see Avison's sacramentalism as what Teselle terms "traditional Christian sacramentalism, deriving from Gnosticism and a Johannine Word-flesh Christology [which] has thought in terms of things that refer to their transcendent counterparts in a static relationship. The pattern is Platonic, two-levelled, and non-temporal." Sallie McFague Teselle, *Literature and the Christian Life*. Yale Publications in Religion 12 (New Haven: Yale UP, 1966), 36.

2. Alan Watts, *Myth and Ritual in Christianity* (London: Thames and Hudson, 1954), 83; Watson E. Mills, "Fish," *The New International Dictionary of the Christian Church*, 377.

3. The words "cropping-clay" are used to express the idea of communion in "Person," *Winter Sun / The Dumbfounding*, 146.

4. D.M.R. Bentley, "Drawers of Water; Notes on the Significance and Scenery of Fresh Water in Canadian Poetry," *CV/ II*, 6, no.4, (Aug. 1982), 28.

5. Klus, 17.

6. Chad Walsh, "A Hope for Literature," *The Climate of Faith in Modern Literature*, ed. Nathan A. Scott, Jr. (New York: Seabury, 1964), 230.

7. Gerard Manley Hopkins, "God's Grandeur," *Poems and Prose of Gerard Manley Hopkins,* ed. W.H. Gardner (Markham: Penguin, 1963), 27.

8. Tesselle, 100.

9. Robert James Merrett, "Faithful Unpredictability: Syntax and Theology in Margaret Avison's Poetry," *"Lighting up the terrain" : The Poetry of Margaret Avison*, ed. David Kent (Toronto: ECW Press, 1987), 99

10. Shakespeare, *The Tempest,* act 1, sc. 2, lines 397-405.

11. Merrett, 99.

12. Hopkins, "God's Grandeur."

13. Shakespeare, *King Lear*, act 4, sc.1, lines 36-37.

14. Margaret Avison, "Perspective," *Poetry of Mid-Century: 1940 / 1960,* New Canadian Library 4, ed. Milton Wilson (Toronto: McClelland and Stewart, 1964), 87-88.

15. See George Ferguson, *Signs & Symbols in Christian Art* (London: Oxford UP, 1961), and/or Redekop. The typology is standard.

16. For an unfortunate misreading of this poem, see Robert James Merrett, "Faithful Unpredictability: Syntax and Theology in Margaret Avison's Poetry," 99, where he makes the

claim that "the worker wrenches the hydrant open to *wash off the 'oils of sun'*" [emphasis mine]. Considering Avison's consistent use of oil and sun imagery throughout her poetry, this reading is insupportable.

17. See both J.M. Kertzer, "Margaret Avison: Power, Knowledge and the Language of Poetry," and Ernest H. Redekop, "sun/Son light/Light: Avison's elemental *Sunblue*," for discussions of Avison's use of the sun symbol. Of interest is David Lyle Jeffrey, "Light, Stillness and the Shaping Word: Conversion and the Poetic of Margaret Avison, *"Lighting up the terrain" : The Poetry of Margaret Avison,* ed. David Kent (Toronto: ECW Press, 1987), 68-69.

18. John 10:9. See my article on "Person" for extensive treatment of this theme.

19. Thomas Molnar, *The Pagan Temptation* (Grand Rapids: Eerdmans, 1987), 179.

20. Steven Olderr, *Symbolism: A Comprehensive Dictionary* (London: McFarland, 1986), 100. He points out that the peacock is both the symbol of "resurrection Easter," and of "eternal life."

21. Douglas John Hall, *Imaging God* (Grand Rapids: Eerdmans, 1986), 116-117. See, in particular, chapters 4, "The Ontology of Communion," and 5, "Being-With-Nature," for further discussions of this theme.

22. Avison, "Perspective."

23. W. Ellwood Post, *Saints, Signs, and Symbols,* 2nd ed. (Wilton, Conn.: Morehouse-Barlow, 1974), 85.

24. Ferguson, 162.

25. Olderr, 65.

26. William Wordsworth, *Tintern Abbey, English Romantic Writers,* ed. David Perkins (New York: Harcourt, 1967), 210.

27. Sir Thomas Wyatt, "I Find no Peace," *The Faber Book of Sonnets,* ed. Robert Nye (London: Faber and Faber, 1976), 35.

28. See W.H. New, "The Mind's Eyes (I's) (Ice): The Poetry of Margaret Avison," *Articulating West: Essays on Purpose and Form in Modern Canadian Literature* (Toronto: New Press, 1972), 234-258.

29. George Herbert, "Love," *Renaissance Poetry,* 2nd ed., ed. Leonard Dean (Englewood Cliffs, N.J.: Prentice-Hall, 1961), 287.

Chapter Two *In The Strong Sun*—(pages 39-57)
1. Hall, 89.

2. *Ibid.,* 120.

3. For the most complete and scholarly treatment of the history of this dogma see, Martin Larson, *The Story of Christian Origins: The Source and Establishment of Western Religion* (Washington, D.C.: Joseph J. Binns, 1977). See also Sallie McFague Tesselle, *Literature and Christian Life.* Yale Publications in Religion 12 (New Haven: Yale UP, 1966).

4. Hall, 98.

5. *Ibid.,* 120.

6. Ernest Redekop, "The Word/word in Avison's Poetry," *"Lighting up the terrain" : The Poetry of Margaret Avison,* ed. David Kent (Toronto: ECW Press, 1987), 126.

7. Klus, 17.

8. See 1 Kings 19:12 where the voice of God is described as "still," and Psalm 46:10, where the psalmist is told to "be still and know that I *am* God."

9. St. Augustine, *The City of God,* trans. Marcus Dods, *The Nicene and Post-Nicene Fathers of The Christian Church,* First Series, ed. Philip Schaff (Grand Rapids: Eerdmans, 1983), 2: 409. " God did not take back all He had imparted to his nature, but something He took and something He left, that there might remain enough to be sensible of the loss of what was taken. And this very sensibility to pain is evidence of the good which has been taken away and the good which has been left."

10. Aide, 70.

11. David Lyle Jeffrey, "Light, Stillness and the Shaping Word: Conversion and the Poetic of Margaret Avison," *"Lighting up the terrain" : The Poetry of Margaret Avison,* ed. David Kent (Toronto: ECW Press, 1987), 67.

12. Ernest Redekop, "sun/Son light/Light," 25; "The Word/word in Avison's Poetry," 125. Here Redekop says that "the fundamental metaphor . . . in all of Avison's poetry—is the *Logos,* the Word made flesh. Jesus is incarnate as reborn language, the original Word of Creation."

13. Ernest Redekop, "The Word/word in Margaret Avison's Poetry," 132.

14. Jaroslav Pelikan, *The Christian Tradition: A History of the Development of Doctrine,* 5 vols. (Chicago: U of Chicago P, 1971), vol.1: *The Emergence of the Catholic Tradition (100-600),* 263-264. This statement, from the "Definition of Chalcedon," which, in 451, updated the Nicene formula, is *the* touchstone of orthodox Christology.

15. Ernest Redekop, "The Word/word in Margaret Avison's Poetry," 132.

16. This sounds very much like modalistic monarchianism, or Sabellianism, to me. Sabellius (c. AD 220) conceived of a "modalistic Trinity according to which God the Father, God the Word, and God the Holy Spirit, exist, not as divisions or

persons in the godhead, but simply as modes of activity. As Father, God manifested Himself as the creator; as Savior, He revealed Himself as the Word or Christ; and now as Comforter, He is present among us as the Holy Spirit. Throughout, God remains unaltered: we have only the differing phases of His *modus operandi.* Thus we have a trinity of successive manifestations, which occur, not simultaneously, but in historic sequence." Martin Larson, *The Story of Christian Origins: The Source and Establishment of Western Religion* (Washington, D.C.: Joseph J. Binns, 1977) 541-542. Jaroslav Pelikan, 179, points out that Sabellius attached "his doctrine to the idea of God as light and the Son of God as radiance." Note Redekop's use of this metaphor in his "sun/Son light/ Light."

17. Lawrence Mathews, "Stevens, Wordsworth, Jesus: Avison and the Romantic Imagination," *"Lighting up the terrain": The Poetry of Margaret Avison,* ed. David Kent (Toronto: ECW Press, 1987), 37.

18. *Ibid.,* 50.

19. Percy Bysshe Shelley, "A Defence of Poetry," *English Romantic Writers,* ed. David Perkins (New York: Harcourt, 1967), 1087.

20. See Thomas Molnar, *The Pagan Temptation* (Grand Rapids: Eerdmans, 1987). See also C. David Mazoff, rev. of *The Pagan Temptation,* by Thomas Molnar, *The Catholic Times* [Montreal] March 1988, 16. Some indispensable sources for understanding the influence of Neoplatonism on Christianity and poetry are M.H. Abrams, *Natural Supernaturalism: Tradition and Revolution in Romantic Literature* (New York: Norton, 1971); and Andrew Louth, *The Origins of the Christian Mystical Tradition: From Plato to Denys* (Toronto: Oxford UP, 1981).

21. Hall, 120.

22. *Ibid.,* 120.

23. See Philippians 2:6-8; see also "Person," *WS/D* 146, and "The Dumbfounding," *WS/D* 152, where clearly the emphasis in on Jesus' humanity, upon His identification with us.

24. Joseph Fitzmyer, *Pauline Theology: A Brief Sketch* (Englewood Cliffs: Prentice-Hall, 1967), 37. "The use of *Kyrios* for Jesus in the early Church bestowed on him the ineffable name of Yahweh in its LXX form. In effect, it suggests that Jesus is on a par with Yahweh himself. This equality is spelled out in detail in the hymn in Phil 2:6-11; the reason why the name given to Jesus is above every name is that it is Yahweh's own name, *Kyrios*" (37).

25. *Ibid.*, 19.

26. *Ibid.*, 22.

27. *Ibid.*, 30-31.

28. We note that the subtitle to "The Circuit" is (Phil 2: 5-11). It is here that "we find the *locus classicus* of Paul's doctrine of the person of Christ and the nature and scope of Christian salvation." R.P. Martin, "Epistle to the Philippians," *The New Bible Dictionary*, 2nd ed., ed. J.D. Douglas et al. (Wheaton, Ill.: Tyndale House, 1982), 931.

29. Ernest Redekop, "The Word/word in Margaret Avison's Poetry," 125.

30. Fitzmyer, 75.

31. William Barnes, "The Garden Wall," *The Poems of William Barnes,* ed. Bernard Jones, 2 vols. (London: Centaur Press, 1962), 2: 774. I thought it might be of interest to compare Avison's poem with the original. Since the poem by Barnes was located only after many hours of tedious search, I have included it in an appendix.

32. The use of the objective correlative in both of these poems reminds one of Tennyson's skilful use of this technique in

"Mariana," *The Major Victorian Poets: Tennyson, Browning, Arnold,* ed. William E. Buckler (New York: Houghton, 1973), 11-13.

33. Milton, *Paradise Lost,* bk. 9, lines 773-784.

34. John 19:34. "The soldier, standing below our crucified Lord as He hung on the cross, would thrust upwards under the left ribs. The broad, clean cutting, two-edged spearhead would enter the distended stomach, would pierce the diaphragm, would cut, wide open, the heart and great blood vessels, arteries and veins now fully distended with blood. . . . The wound would be large enough to permit the open hand to be thrust into it." R.V.G. Tasker, *The Gospel According to St. John: An Introduction and Commentary, The Tyndale New Testament Commentaries,* vol. 4 (Grand Rapids: Eerdmans, 1960), 213.

35. 1 Corinthians 15:3; Galatians 1:4; 1 John 2:2.

36. Andrew Louth, 79-80. "This idea of the soul as a mirror which, when pure, can reflect the image of God seems to be original to Athanasius [although] there are faint hints in Theophilus and Plotinus. . . . The idea of the soul as a mirror reflecting God is thus for the Fathers . . . a metaphor that sees the soul as [a] real, though dependent, image of God and also suggests that this image of God in the soul is perceived in self-knowledge." Louth also traces the development of this idea through Gregory of Nyssa, who held that "because the soul is a mirror reflecting the divine image, the soul can contemplate God by contemplating the divine image present within itself," 91, and St. Augustine, whence it passed into Western thought.

37. Leon Morris, *The First Epistle of Paul to the Corinthians, The Tyndale New Testament Commentaries,* vol. 7 (Grand Rapids: Eerdmans, 1960), 188.

38. "Her jobs . . . have included inner-city social work and secretarial work in the Canadian office of a Southeast Asia mission." Information taken from the cover of *sunblue.*

39. Wolfgang Iser, *The Act of Reading: A Theory of Aesthetic Response* (Baltimore and London: Johns Hopkins UP, 1978), 163-167.

40. Rod Willmot, "Winning Spirit," rev. of *sunblue,* by Margaret Avison. *Canadian Literature* 89 (Winter 1980), 116.

41. Raymond Souster, "Roller Skate Man," *Canadian Anthology,* ed. Carl F. Klinck, 3rd ed. (Toronto: Gage, 1974), 467-468. In order to facilitate a comparison by the reader, I have included this poem in an appendix.

42. Exodus 16:12-15.

43. John 6:31-35; 48-51. See also Alan Watts, *Myth and Ritual in Christianity*, 93.

44. 2 Cor. 4:7.

45. The reference here is to Moses smiting the rock, Num. 20:11; the allusion is to our desire to hit God, and, by extension, to the crucifixion.

46. Romans 9:21-23.

47. Iser, 227.

48. Luke 10: 38-42. The story of Rita and Vivian has thematic similarities with this episode.

Chapter Three *Restoration*—(pages 58-69)
1. Watts, 206-207.

2. Revelation 21:1.

3. Revelation 10:6.

4. Mircea Eliade, *The Sacred and the Profane: The Nature of Religion,* trans, Willard R. Trask (New York: Harcourt, 1959), 68-112.

5. See Molnar for a full explication of this idea.

6. Louth, 76-77. The Platonic idea that the soul had kinship with the divine and that souls were not created but pre-existent was undone at Nicaea through the doctrine of *creatio ex nihilo* which "implies that the most fundamental ontological divide is not between the spiritual and the material but between God and the created order, to which latter both soul and body belong. The soul has nothing in common with God; there is no kinship between it and the divine."

7. Larson, 103.

8. Michael Grant and John Hazel, *Who's Who in Classical Mythology* (New York: Hodder and Stoughton, 1979), 114-115.

9. See also Colossians 1:27.

10. bpNichol, "Sketching," *"Lighting up the terrain": The Poetry of Margaret Avison,* ed. David Kent (Toronto: ECW Press, 1987), 112-113. Nichol obviously considers "Bereaved" to be a SKETCH poem. He points out that "SKETCH poems move from a noting of detail . . . . to the sudden change of perception," a movement that describes the activity of "Bereaved."

11. Robert James Merrett, "Faithful Unpredictability: Syntax and Theology in Margaret Avison's Poetry," 109.

12. bpNichol, p. 113.

13." Ziggurat," *The Oxford Companion to Art,* 1970.

14. Genesis 11:28, 31. One notes that Ur was in Babylon, (*Babel*, "gate of god"). D. J. Wiseman, "Babel," *The New Bible Dictionary*, 2nd ed., ed. J.D. Douglas et al. (Wheaton, Ill.: Tyndale House, 1982), 110. "The history of the building of the city and its lofty tower is given in Gen.11: 1-11, where

the name Babel is explained by popular etymology based on a similar Heb. root *balal*, as 'confusion' or 'mixing'. Babel thus became a synonym for the confusion caused by language differences which was part of the divine punishment for the human pride displayed in the building."

15. Hopkins, 27.

16. Ephesians 2:6.

17. Romans 9:28-39.

18. David Kent, "Introduction," *"Lighting up the terrain":The Poetry of Margaret Avison,* ed. David Kent (Toronto: ECW Press, 1987), iv.

19. *Ibid.,* v.

20. Margaret Avison, "Muse of Danger," *"Lighting up the terrain": The Poetry of Margaret Avison,* ed. David Kent (Toronto: ECW Press, 1987), 144.

21. *Ibid.,* 146.

22. *Ibid.,* 145.

23. *Ibid.,* 146.

24. I am referring to the negative reception of *sunblue* by Messrs. Willmot and Scobie.

25. Avison, "Muse of Danger," 147.

26. *Ibid.,* 147.

BIBLIOGRAPHY

Primary Sources

Avison, Margaret. *The Dumbfounding*. New York: Norton, 1966.

———. "Muse of Danger," in David Kent, ed., *"Lighting up the Terrain": The Poetry of Margaret Avison*. Toronto: ECW Press, 1987.

———. "Person." *Winter Sun / The Dumbfounding*. Toronto: McClelland and Stewart, 1982.

———. *sunblue*. Hantsport, Nova Scotia: Lancelot Press, 1978.

———. *Winter Sun*. Toronto: University of Toronto Press, 1960.

———. *Winter Sun / The Dumbfounding*. Toronto: McClelland and Stewart, 1982.

Secondary Sources
Books

Abrams, M.H. *Natural Supernaturalism: Tradition and Revolution in Romantic Literature*. New York: Norton, 1971.

The Bible. King James Version.

Douglas, J. D., ed. *The New International Dictionary of the Christian Church.* Grand Rapids: Zondervan, 1974.

Douglas, J.D., and Norman Hillyer, eds. *The New Bible Dictionary.* 2nd ed. Wheaton, Illinois: Tyndale House, 1982.

Eliade, Mircea. *The Sacred and the Profane: The Nature of Religion.* Trans. Willard R. Trask. New York: Harcourt, 1959.

Ferguson, George. *Signs & Symbols in Christian Art.* London: Oxford University Press, 1961.

Fitzmyer, Joseph A. *Pauline Theology: A Brief Sketch.* Englewood Cliffs, New Jersey: Prentice-Hall, 1967.

Grant, Michael, and John Hazel. *Who's Who in Classical Mythology.* New York: Hodder and Stoughton, 1979.

Graves, Robert. *The White Goddess: A Historical Grammar of Poetic Myth,* Toronto: McGraw, 1966.

Hall, Douglas John. *Imaging God: Dominion as Stewardship.* Grand Rapids: Eerdmans, 1986.

Hawkes, Terence. *Structuralism and Semiotics.* Berkeley: University of California Press, 1977.

Hazleton, Roger. *A Theological Approach to Art.* New York: Abingdon Press, 1967.

Hirsch, E. D. Jr. *Validity in Interpretation.* New Haven: Yale University Press, 1967.

Iser, Wolfgang. *The Act of Reading: A Theory of Aesthetic Response.* Baltimore and London: John Hopkins University Press, 1978.

Kent, David, ed. *"Lighting up the terrain": The Poetry of Margaret Avison*. Toronto: ECW Press, 1987.

Kermode, Frank, ed. *Selected Prose of T.S. Eliot*. London: Faber, 1975.

Klus, Christopher. "The Religious Poetry of Margaret Avison." Unpublished M.A. thesis, McMaster University, 1972.

Larson, Martin. *The Story of Christian Origins: The Source and Establishment of Western Religion*. Washington, D.C.: Joseph J. Binns, 1977.

Louth, Andrew. *The Origins of the Christian Mystical Tradition: From Plato to Denys*. Toronto: Oxford University Press, 1981.

Milton, John. *Paradise Lost*. Ed. Merritt Y. Hughes. Indianapolis, Ind.: Odyssey Press, 1962.

Molnar, Thomas. *The Pagan Temptation*. Grand Rapids: Eerdmans, 1987.

Morris, Leon. *The First Epistle of Paul to the Corinthians*. Vol 7 of *The Tyndale New Testament Commentaries*. Ed. R.V.G. Tasker. Grand Rapids: Eerdmans, 1960.

Norris, Ken. *The Little Magazine in Canada 1925-80*. Toronto: ECW Press, 1984.

Olderr, Steven. *Symbolism: A Comprehensive Dictionary*. London: McFarland, 1986.

Partridge, A.C. *The Language of Modern Poetry: Yeats, Eliot, Auden*. London: Andre Deutsch, 1976.

Pelikan, Jaroslav. *The Emergence of the Catholic Tradition (100-600)*. Vol 1 of *The Christian Tradition: A History of the Development of Doctrine*. 5 Vols. Chicago: University of Chicago Press, 1971.

Post, W. Ellwood. *Saints, Signs, and Symbols*. 2nd ed. Wilton, Conn.: Morehouse-Barlow, 1974.

Redekop, Ernest. *Margaret Avison*. Studies in Canadian Literature 9. Toronto: Copp Clark, 1970.

St. Augustine. *The City of God*. Trans. Marcus Dods. *The Nicene and Post-Nicene Fathers of the Christian Church*. First Series. Ed. Philip Schaff. Grand Rapids: Eerdmans, 1983. Vol.2.

St. Pierre, Jeannette. "Avison and the Metaphysicals." Unpublished M.A. thesis, McMaster University,1982.

Schaeffer, Francis A. *How Then Should We Live? The Rise and Decline of Western Thought and Culture*. Westchester, Ill.: Crossway Books, 1976.

Scott, Nathan A., Jr. *The Broken Center: Studies in the Theological Horizon of Modern Literature*. The William Lyon Phelps Lectures, 1965. New Haven: Yale University Press, 1966.

——. *Negative Capability: Studies in the New Literature and the Religious Situation*. New Haven: Yale University Press, 1969.

——, ed. *The Climate of Faith in Modern Literature*. New York: Seabury Press, 1964.

——. *The New Orpheus: Essays toward a Christian Poetic*. New York: Sheed and Ward, 1964.

Shakespeare, William. *The Riverside Shakespeare*. Ed. G. Blakemore Evans. Boston: Houghton, 1974.

Tasker, R.V.G. *The Gospel According to St. John: An Introduction and Commentary*. Vol 4 of *The Tyndale New Testament Commentaries*. Grand Rapids, Michigan: Eerdmans, 1964.

Teselle, Sallie McFague. *Literature and the Christian Life.* Yale Publications in Religion 12. New Haven: Yale University Press, 1966.

Tillich, Paul. *Systematic Theology.* 3 vols. Chicago: University of Chicago Press, 1963.

———. *Theology of Culture.* Ed. Robert C. Kimball. New York: Oxford University Press, 1959.

Turnell, Martin. *Modern Literature and Christian Faith.* Westminster, Md.: Newman Press, 1961.

Watts, Alan. *Myth and Ritual in Christianity.* London: Thames and Hudson, 1954.

Weiss, Paul. *Religion and Art.* The Aquinas Lecture, 1963. Milwaukee: Marquette University Press, 1963.

Wilder, Amos N. *Theology and Modern Literature.* William Belden Noble Lectures, 1956. Cambridge: Harvard University Press, 1958.

Williamson, Hendrika. "Man and Mandala: The Poetry of Margaret Avison." Unpublished M.A. thesis, Simon Fraser University, 1970.

Wilson, Milton, ed. *Poetry of Mid-Century: 1940 / 1960.* New Canadian Library 4. Toronto: McClelland and Stewart, 1964.

Secondary Sources
Articles, Poems, Stories
Aide, William. "An Immense Answering of Human Skies: The Poetry of Margaret Avison," in David Helwig, ed.,*The Human Elements,* 2nd series. Ottawa: Oberon Press, 1981, 51-76.

Barnes, William. "The Garden Wall," in Bernard Jones, ed., *The Poems of William Barnes*. London: Centaur Press, 1962, vol. 2, 774.

Bellow, Saul. "The Gonzaga Manuscripts," in Douglas Angus and Sylvia Angus, eds., *Contemporary American Short Stories*. New York: Fawcett Premier, 1967, 387-418.

Bentley, D.M.R. "Drawers of Water; Notes on the Significance and Scenery of Fresh Water in Canadian Poetry," *CV/II*, 6 no.4 (August 1982), 27-28.

Bowering, George. "Avison's Imitation of Christ the Artist," *A Way with Words*. Toronto: Oberon Press, 1982, 5-23.

Doerkson, Daniel W. "Search and Discovery: Margaret Avison's Poetry,"in George Woodcock, ed., *Poets and Critics: Essays from Canadian Literature 1966-1974*. Toronto: Oxford University Press, 1974, 123-137.

Eliot, T. S. "Religion and Literature," in Frank Kermode, ed., *Selected Prose of T.S. Eliot*. London: Faber, 1975, 97-106.

Geddes, G., and Phyllis Bruce, eds. "Notes on the Poets." *15 Canadian Poets*. Toronto: Oxford University Press, 1970, 266-268.

Herbert, George. "Love," in Leonard Dean, ed., *Renaissance Poetry*. 2nd ed. Englewood Cliffs, N.J.: Prentice-Hall, 1961, 287.

Hopkins, Gerard Manley. "God's Grandeur," in W.H. Gardner, ed., *Poems and Prose of Gerard Manley Hopkins*. Markham: Penguin, 1963, 27.

Jeffrey, David Lyle. "Light, Stillness and the Shaping Word: Conversion and the Poetic of Margaret Avison," in David Kent, ed., *"Lighting up the terrain" : The Poetry of Margaret Avison.* Toronto: ECW Press, 1987, 58-77.

Johnston, George. "Avison's Temple." Review of *sunblue, Canadian Forum* (May 1979), 30-31.

Jones, Lawrence M. "A Core of Brilliance: Margaret Avison's Achievement." *Canadian Literature* 38 (1968), 51.

Kent, David. "Introduction," in David Kent, ed., *"Lighting up the terrain" : The Poetry of Margaret Avison.* listed above, i-x.

Kertzer, J. M. "Margaret Avison: Power, Knowledge and the Language of Poetry," *Canadian Poetry: Studies, Documents, Reviews* 4 (Spring-Summer 1979), 29-44.

———. "Margaret Avison,"in Jeffrey M. Heath, ed., *Profiles in Canadian Literature*, 6 vols. Toronto: Dunburn Press, 1980, 2, 33-40.

Mansbridge, Francis. "Margaret Avison: An Annotated Bibliography," in Robert Lecker and Jack David, eds., *The Annotated Bibliography of Canada's Major Authors.* 6 vols. Toronto: ECW Press, 1985, 6, 13-66.

Martin, R.P. "Epistle to the Philippians," in J.D. Douglas et al, eds., *The New Bible Dictionary.* 2nd ed. Wheaton, Ill.: Tyndale House, 1982, 931.

Mathews, Lawrence. "Stevens, Wordsworth, Jesus: Avison and the Romantic Imagination," in David Kent, ed., *"Lighting up the terrain" : The Poetry of Margaret Avison.* listed above, 36-54.

Mazoff, C. D. Review of *The Pagan Temptation*, by Thomas Molnar. *The Catholic Times* [Montreal] (March. 1988), 16.

———. "Through the Son: An Explication of Margaret Avison's 'Person'." *Canadian Poetry: Studies, Documents, Reviews* 22 (Spring-Summer 1988), 40-48.

McNally, Paul. Review of *sunblue*, *The Fiddlehead* 123 (Fall 1979), 100-102.

Merrett, Robert James. "Faithful Unpredictability: Syntax and Theology in Margaret Avison's Poetry," in David Kent, ed., *"Lighting up the terrain": The Poetry of Margaret Avison*, listed above, 82-110.

———. "The Ominous Centre: The Theological Impulse in Margaret Avison's Poetry." *White Pelican* 5.2 (1976), 12-24.

Mills, Ralph J., Jr. "The Voice of the Poet in the Modern City," in Nathan A. Scott, ed., *The Climate of Faith in Modern Literature*. New York: Seabury, 1964, 142-176.

Mills, Watson E. "Fish," in J.D. Douglas, ed., *The New International Dictionary of the Christian Church*. Grand Rapids: Zondervan, 1974, 377.

Moritz, Albert. "Stalking the Sacred Asparagus." Review of *sunblue*, *Books in Canada* (August-September 1979), 28-29.

New, W.H. "The Mind's Eyes (I's) (Ice): The Poetry of Margaret Avison." *Articulating West: Essays on Purpose and Form in Modern Canadian Literature*. Toronto: New Press, 1972, 234-258.

Newman, Robert C. "Natural Theology," in J.D. Douglas, ed., *The New International Dictionary of the Christian Church*. Grand Rapids: Zondervan, 1974.

Nichol, bp. "Sketching," in David Kent, ed., *"Lighting up the terrain": The Poetry of Margaret Avison,* listed above, 111-115.

Redekop, Ernest. "sun/Son light/Light: Avison's elemental *Sunblue." Canadian Poetry: Studies, Documents, Reviews* 7 (1980), 21-37.

———. "The Word/word in Avison's Poetry," in David Kent, ed., *"Lighting up the terrain": The Poetry of Margaret Avison,* listed above, 115-143.

Ross, Malcolm. "The Writer as Christian," in Nathan A. Scott Jr., ed., *The New Orpheus: Essays toward a Christian Poetic*. New York: Sheed and Ward, 1964, 83-93.

Rougemont, Denis de. "Religion and the Mission of the Artist," in Nathan A. Scott Jr., ed., *The New Orpheus: Essays toward a Christian Poetic,* listed above, 59-73.

Scobie, Stephen. Review of *sunblue, Queen's Quarterly* 87 (Spring 1980), 158-160.

Shelly, Percy Bysshe. "A Defence of Poetry," in David Perkins, ed., *English Romantic Writers*. New York: Harcourt, 1967, 1072-1087.

Souster, Raymond. "Roller Skate Man," in Carl F. Klinck, ed., *Canadian Anthology,* 3rd ed., rev. and enl. Toronto: Gage, 1974, 467-468.

Tennyson, Alfred Lord. "Mariana," in William E. Buckler, ed., *The Major Victorian Poets: Tennyson, Browning, Arnold.* New York: Houghton, 1973, 11-13.

Wallace, Ronald S. "Sacrament," in J.D. Douglas, ed., *The New International Dictionary of the Christian Church,* listed above.

Walsh, Chad. "A Hope for Literature," in Nathan A. Scott, Jr., ed., *The Climate of Faith in Modern Literature,* listed above, 207-233.

Willmot, Rod. "Winning Spirit." Review of *sunblue, Canadian Literature 89* (Winter 1980), 115-116.

Wiseman, D. J. "Babel," in J.D. Douglas et al, eds., *The New Bible Dictionary,* listed above, 110-111.

Woodcock, George. "Poetry," in Carl F. Klinck et al, eds., *Literary History of Canada: Canadian Literature in English,* 2nd ed. 3 vols. Toronto: University of Toronto Press, 1976. Vol. 3: 284-317.

Wordsworth, William. "Tintern Abbey," in David Perkins, ed., *English Romantic Writers.* New York: Harcourt, 1967, 209-211.

Wyatt, Sir Thomas. "I Find No Peace," in Robert Nye, ed., *The Faber Book of Sonnets.* London: Faber and Faber, 1976, 35.

"Ziggurat." *The Oxford Companion to Art.* Ed. Harold Osborne. Oxford: Oxford University Press, 1970.

APPENDIX

The Garden Wall

By the rock the water leapeth,
By the elm the wind-blast sweepeth,
Where at night the milch cow sleepeth,
   While, as yet, no leaves may fall;
Round the dell the roadway bendeth,
O'er the fields the footpath wendeth,
Glades begin where woodland endeth
   Far without the garden wall.

Where he will the rider flitteth,
Turning by the roads he witteth;
When he will the walker sitteth
   Where some cool-air'd shade may fall;
But though ev'ry passer spieth
Field and house, as on he hieth,
'Tis not ev'ry one that prieth
   There within the garden wall.

There the ruddy apple groweth,
There the sweetsmell'd blossom bloweth,
There the blushing maiden goeth,
   Fairer than the rose's ball.
Blest is he whose time onfleeteth,
Far too fast, whe'er he meeteth
Smiles from her, as ther she greeteth
   Him within the garden wall.

Roller Skate Man

A freak of the city,
little man with big head,
shrivelled body, stumps of legs
clamped to a block of wood
running on roller-skate wheels.

On his hands gloves
because the Queen Street pavements
are rough when your hands are paddles
and you speed between
silk-stockinged legs
and extravagant pleats,

steering through familiar waters
of spit, old butts, chewed gum,
flotsam among the jetsam of your world.

INDEX